DeRo

DeRo

My Life

DWAYNE DE ROSARIO

WITH BRENDAN DUNLOP

Editor for the Press: Michael Holmes
Cover design: Michel Vrana
Cover photograph by Heather Pollock

LIBRARY AND ARCHIVES CANADA CATALOGUING IN PUBLICATION

Title: DeRo : my life / Dwayne De Rosario with Brendan Dunlop.

Names: De Rosario, Dwayne, author. | Dunlop, Brendan, author.

Identifiers: Canadiana (print) 20200403990 | Canadiana (ebook) 20200404008

ISBN 978-1-77041-527-0 (HARDCOVER)
ISBN 978-1-77305-663-0 (EPUB)
ISBN 978-1-77305-664-7 (PDF)
ISBN 978-1-77305-665-4 (Kindle)

Subjects: LCSH: De Rosario, Dwayne. | LCSH: Soccer players—Canada—Biography. | LCGFT: Autobiographies.

Classification: LCC GV942.7.D42 A3 2021 | DDC 796.334092—dc23

ISBN 978-1-77305-759-0 (AUDIO)

The publication of *DeRo: My Life* is funded in part by the Government of Canada. *Ce livre est financé en partie par le gouvernement du Canada.* We also acknowledge the support of the Government of Ontario through the Ontario Book Publishing Tax Credit, and through Ontario Creates for the marketing of this book.

PRINTED AND BOUND IN CANADA

PRINTING: FRIESENS 5 4 3 2 1

CHAPTER 1

STARTED FROM THE BOTTOM

Ask anyone around the world what they think about Toronto, and they'll hit you with all the clichés.

It's a world class city.

It's so diverse.

Everyone gets along with each other.

There's hardly any crime.

I could see myself living there.

Ask anyone about Scarborough, where I grew up, and you'll get a very different reaction.

It's not safe out there, man.

Everybody's got a gun.

Don't drive out there if you like your car because it will get stolen, for sure.

Anyone that tells you that hasn't spent any real time in Scarborough. Located in the east end of Toronto — although during rush-hour traffic it can feel twice as far away from downtown than it actually is — it can feel light-years away from the upper-class, global city the world has come to love. But in a lot of ways, Scarborough is the best representation of Canada: it's a diverse, hard-working community filled with proud new Canadians.

Scarborough was like every other poor community. It could either make you or break you. And there were more ways to break you.

There weren't after-school programs and activities to keep kids busy when school was let out. Most kids weren't picked up by Mom and driven to some class or music lesson. Most of the boys weren't going home to a well-prepared meal every day.

Instead, most kids walked home alone to an empty apartment. If they wanted to eat, they better have learned how to make dinner themselves. Many kids went to bed before their parents got home from work, if that's where they even were or if they were lucky to have a parent who had a job. Imagine yourself in that situation as an eight-year-old. What would you do?

Our apartment was never empty. And it was never quiet. Music always brought us together. We'd wake up every morning to my dad playing his vinyls or cassettes. Soul. R&B. Lovers rock. Reggae. Music was always playing. It was instrumental in my life, and I take it with me wherever I go. It was music that helped me keep my sanity growing up. It was music that was my escape.

Music reminded me of when my parents were together. They split up when I was five years old. No divorce is easy when there are children involved, and I don't blame them. They had married young. My parents immigrated to Canada from Guyana in 1973 when my brother Paul was born. Then they had Mark. And then me. They were young Caribbean parents trying to make it in a new country, against the odds. I'll never know the truth about why it didn't work, and that's not for me to know. But their divorce wasn't easy for anyone.

We were forced to choose. My brothers chose to live with my dad, and I didn't want to be split up from my brothers, so I chose Dad too. I'll never forget the look on my mother's face. She was completely heartbroken. She had lost her partner, and now she had lost all three sons. That walk out of the courtroom was the loneliest moment of her life. I don't remember much from those court battles — maybe I've just deleted that stuff from my memory. It was such a blow to go from our

In loving memory of my father
John Anthony De Rosario

TABLE OF CONTENTS

FOREWORD

You can pick an athlete out of a crowd, usually just by their body structure, but there's also an attitude about them that typically stands out. You can pick a champion out of a crowd of athletes by their swagger. They have this aura about them that is just different than everybody else.

I first met DeRo at the ESPY Awards. Two things caught my eye on the red carpet that night: Floyd Mayweather's crew of security guards and Dwayne's flashy jacket. It reminded me of the Teddy Boy style back in England during the 1950s. The man has always had his own flare, on and off the field. And he's still got skills.

I watched him play an indoor game a few years ago, and he scored five goals. I guess I was impressed because he must have been the oldest player out there. But DeRo is a champion. That's just what I expect from him.

Over the years we've become good friends. He reminds me a lot of myself. Introduced to each other as champions, we share a similar love for music, business, and fatherhood. The world knows us for what we did while at the top of the sports world, but our kids just know us as their dads. They are our world now.

When my time comes to knock on heaven's door, and God asks, "What did you do with your life?" I want to be able to show more than just the world titles and what I did wearing boxing gloves. I want to leave a legacy. Dwayne is the same way. The two of us are like fine wine: we get better with time.

He built a legacy on the field and is now building one that his children, his country, and his community can be proud of. Dwayne is a Canadian diamond. And when you have one to look at every day, you don't realize how valuable it is. I don't think people know how big Dwayne's heart is.

To surprise me on my birthday one year, he flew my favourite reggae artist, Maxi Priest, to Toronto, to play at my party. I have met a lot of musicians and rock stars in my day, but I had never met him. Dwayne knew that, so Dwayne made it happen.

Everything he's wanted in life, he's had to make happen for himself. DeRo's life isn't a sad story. It's a great story. And there are too many sad stories out there in the world right now.

While reading this book, you'll see that just because you struggle, doesn't mean you can't still triumph. It wasn't easy for DeRo to get to the top of the soccer world, but he did. And that's just one part of his great story.

—LENNOX LEWIS, THREE-TIME WORLD
HEAVYWEIGHT BOXING CHAMPION, CM CBE

PROLOGUE

"Yo, DeRo, I want to show you something."

He reached into his school bag and pulled out a gun.

"What the fuck are you gonna do with that?" I asked him.

Real tough guys didn't carry guns. Nobody in my crew had a gun, and none of the gangs we scrapped with did either. So who the hell did this guy think he was?

"I'll shoot anybody that looks at me funny," he joked.

"You wouldn't shoot anybody, man. You're a bitch," I said, laughing. As he squared up to me, I could see in his face that my attitude was really starting to piss him off. "I ain't scared of no tall kid with a fake gun!"

I wasn't scared of anybody. He looked down at the gun in his hand and started chuckling to himself.

"You're a bitch!" I said again. He was mad now.

He looked up at me and pointed the gun to my head.

I laughed at him. He was testing me, but I wasn't afraid. The gun was cold against my forehead and I could feel its weight.

"Call me a 'bitch' again, and I'm gonna pull the trigger!"

When you're a young teen, you don't fear death. I was more afraid he thought he could bully me and get away with it.

"Bro, you're a bitch!"

Bang.

happy five-person home in Malvern, a neighbourhood in Scarborough, to a one-bedroom apartment at Kennedy Road and Eglinton Avenue.

Auntie Lea took us in. She was my dad's mother's sister. Auntie had the bedroom, and she let me sleep in the bed with her most nights. My brothers swapped between a cot and the living room floor, and Dad slept on the couch. Her building was one of many government-housing blocks in the area. The tap water was grey. There was no air-conditioning. People set off the fire alarms almost every night. And the elevators never worked. But moving in with Auntie Lea would become one of the biggest blessings of my life.

Born in 1905, Lea was the oldest of seven siblings. After their parents died when the children were young, Lea and her brothers and sisters were forced to live in a convent in Guyana, where Lea took care of the family. What I was going through was nothing compared to what she had lived through.

From the day we moved in, my dad worked his ass off. That left my Aunt to bear the brunt of trying to control three wild kids in a tough environment. She took to me, and I really took to her. I think she saw the talent in me before I even saw it in myself. She was my angel.

My first few years of school were difficult because I spoke differently than the other kids. I had picked up Auntie's thick Guyanese accent. School was never my priority, and I was a real shit disturber in the classroom. I would egg the boys on to cause trouble and make the day a nightmare for the teacher. You know in cartoons when a character has a choice to make, and he's got a little angel on one shoulder and a little devil on the other? I was the little devil. Always.

One time in grade 6, I drove this teacher bananas. He turned around and threw a piece of chalk at me. It hit me in the foot and messed up my white Nikes. I couldn't believe it. The whole class was stunned. Every ghetto kid knows, you need the freshest kicks. I needed those Jordans, those Ewings, those K-Swiss, that Champion tracksuit. It was status. You had to look fly at school. So I picked up the chalk and threw it right back at him. Hit him right in the forehead. I couldn't have thrown it that well again if I had another 10 tries.

I had a bad temper growing up. My brothers and I would fight like we were WWE wrestlers, throwing each other around the apartment like rag dolls, trying to bounce off the back of the sofa like the ropes in the ring, and kicking each other in the stomach before dropping a suplex in the middle of the living room. My older brothers loved kicking my ass, and they did all the time. This is definitely where my hatred for losing came from.

And I don't just hate losing, I'm a sore loser. I don't think that's a bad thing. You appreciate winning so much that you can't stand losing. Growing up, it got me in more trouble than I needed. The neighbourhood basketball court was a multi-sport arena for my brothers and me: part basketball court, part boxing ring.

One time we played basketball and they just destroyed me. It didn't matter how hard I tried, how fast I ran, or where I shot from, they destroyed me. They had the obvious advantage of being older and taller, but that wasn't an excuse for me. I was so angry, I picked up a piece of broken glass from the side of the court and threw it at my brother standing 10 feet away. I hit him right in the calf. Man, I had never felt so bad and so scared at the same time. I knew he was going to beat my ass for days and never let me live that down. And I knew my dad was going to beat my ass for hurting my brother because I couldn't control my temper.

He was fine. He needed a few stitches, but we were playing on that court again in no time. Broken glass and my temper were a constant on that court. Eventually, I grew up to not be so malicious when I got angry. As a pro, I always felt like it was my fault if we lost. Even if it was a defender or a goalkeeper that had made the mistake, I put it on me. There was something I should've done earlier. There was something I could have done better so that their mistake didn't have as big of an effect on that game.

Both my passion and my love of soccer comes from my dad. When he wasn't working or driving us around, he was playing. He helped form this team called Kendall United. They played in the T&D League, a Caribbean men's league. What I took most from that experience was the community. It brought families together and united not only Guyanese Canadians like us, but the whole community. Everyone came out to see the moves, and the tricks. Anyone who's been to a Caribbean game has seen the craziest shit. There were more fights at those games than there were in the NHL back then. One time my dad was the goalkeeper, and he was so angry with his own team yelling at each other and yelling at him, he kicked the ball into his own net.

"Hear tek dis! Go long, go fetch de ball and play goal if yuh nuh happy!" That was his way of kissing his teeth to say "see what you did! Now they're winning! Shut up and go get that goal back!"

It was a funny way of motivating.

My Auntie raised us, but the streets made us the kids we were. In my neighbourhood, "crew life" wasn't a way to live. It was the *only* way.

We called ourselves crews because we weren't gangs. We rolled in a group, made a mess of things everywhere we went, and always got up to no good with other groups of kids. But we weren't a gang.

My crew was called "Boys in Blue" and we were rebels, like how the punk kids were in England. And our crew wasn't just made up of Black boys and Caribbean kids. Like Scarborough, my crew was as mixed as could be. We loved that it made us different than a lot of the other groups in the projects. It worked to our advantage. The African kids didn't want to cross us once they saw how wild our Africans were, same with the Latinos. Being diverse helped quash a lot of beefs that really could have gotten out of hand.

We were the kids that your parents told you not to hang around. Each school day was another day to get up to some shit we just hoped we could get away with. Our teachers couldn't control us, and our parents didn't have a plan. So we just wanted to burn the house down.

We felt like warriors. You couldn't go a week without getting into a fight at my school. If there wasn't a reason to scrap, you'd find one. We would actually schedule times to fight.

Boys in Blue would meet up at Kennedy Station. That was our base. We'd take the subway and ride two buses for an hour to meet a group of kids we didn't like. Then the next week or the week after, if they hadn't had enough, they'd come out to Scarborough and get stomped. It's funny how fair we were to do it "home and away." We only knew these kids because we played futsal tournaments against them. But we didn't play half as many soccer games against those kids as we planned fights.

Fighting against that crew gave us a lot of confidence because we were younger, and we'd usually win. Even though we wanted to smash each other's heads in, we respected each other, so things never got to the point that it would end up in the newspaper.

What's the motivation to fight all the time? We hardly had anything better to do. There were no weapons. It was just throwback schoolyard scrapping. And everybody was there to protect each other. My brothers were there, so I had to go to protect them. I didn't really think about getting hurt. It didn't matter if you were my best friend. If you hit my brother, I was gonna knock you out. Other guys that knew we were fighters would start a beef for no reason because they knew we'd join in and do the fighting for them. Countless times we wouldn't even know what started the fight, but when we'd find out, we'd think, "Seriously? That's what we were fighting about?"

There was always someone else crazy enough to start it off. I didn't have to be the big man on the frontline. One crew member would pick out the loudest kid, walk straight up to him, and crack him with a head-butt. "Let's go! I don't give a shit!"

We all had that mentality. I used to slide into a guy, take his feet out, and then start beating on him. I would get a few jabs in here and there but I didn't have to be that one-on-one boxer type of guy.

It wasn't always like that though. Sometimes, the crew would just be at a basement party and some kid from another hood would start something, so we'd have to fuck shit up.

We beat up some kid really bad this one time. I don't remember why, but I remember his eyes were so swollen he could barely see when he left. At the time you didn't fear the consequences; you just knew you'd have to deal with them at some point.

A few days later there was this big school party, and sure enough his older brothers rolled up on me and my two brothers. Paul wanted to have a good night. He didn't want these idiots to ruin it, so he pushed Mark and me back and said, "I'm gonna take care of this!" We didn't listen.

We all ran straight towards the biggest guy. He reached to grab something out of his belt. I didn't know if it was a knife or a bottle, but I knew these guys were seriously looking to hurt us. Paul kicked him right in his chest, like Jean-Claude Van Damme. Mark and I just kept running. We split up, and the other guys chased after us.

That was the most scared I'd ever been. I didn't stop running until I got to Kennedy Station, which was at least 20 minutes away. I hated messing up my nice kicks. We were supposed to have a good night but . . .

There were no cell phones back then, so you just had to wait for the crew to show up again. That shit messes with your mind. Nobody could do that now. I had a pager and paced around the whole station, waiting for Paul to beep me. Finally, he did. I was so relieved. I didn't know where he was, but I knew he got away too.

Once, some eighth graders did something to some kids at Midland High School. Their ninth and tenth graders came to our school looking for payback. My brother was in grade 8, and even though he didn't have anything to do with it, he was fighting. And if my brother was fighting, I was fighting. These high school kids rolled up to start trouble at a middle school, and all these kids three or four years younger were out in numbers, ready to fight.

Now, police officers roam the hallways or sit in their patrol cars when school gets out. Back then, all that responsibility was on the teachers and the staff. Our principal punched one of those high school kids in the face. I'm sure he felt justified at the time and believed that he had no other option. That's how I felt watching him fight. But these were the examples of leadership we grew up seeing. Fighting might not have been the best answer, but you sure as hell couldn't come up with a better one in the moment.

———

When I was 12, we moved into a two-bedroom apartment at Victoria Park Avenue and Lawrence Avenue. Our penthouse in the sky. The water was cleaner, and there was a maintained court close by we could play ball at. My brothers and I were so excited to finally have our own room. The three of us had to share it, but it was the biggest advancement for us. We at least had some privacy to scheme up some trouble while we drifted off to sleep.

Breakdancing would keep us busy after school for hours. My nickname in that world was "Timex" and my brother Paul went by "Pace." He started a crew called SuperNaturalz with Curtis, Jedi, Reviere, LegO, and Ninja. They were the best breakdancers in Toronto. They used to battle Bag of Tricks, Paranormal, and other crews in parking lots and at train stations. We were keeping the breakdancing scene alive, living life like a music video. For some of us, it was a much-needed outlet, a way to express ourselves outside of our family. Regardless of all the trouble we were getting into, we had some good times.

The more athletic you were, the more daring you could be. Some dancer would pull off a move that nobody had ever seen before that would just blow our minds. And then someone would come flying in with a kung fu kick because they were pissed that they didn't bust out that move first. Cue the brawl. While everyone would be brawling and scrapping, it was some kid's job to run the boom box to safety like it was a baby.

This DJ called "Funky Joe" used to work our school dances. My boys and I thought we could easily do what this guy was doing. So we put a mix tape together and slapped it on the principal's desk with so much confidence, like one of these kids today with two million Instagram followers.

Bam! "Stop paying Funky Joe and start paying us!"

He looked at us like, "Who the hell do these little kids think they are?"

I don't know how we would've done it. We didn't have any equipment, and we had only a few records. I used to go down to Melo Music. He had all the vintage stuff. To get the new stuff and hip-hop, we had to go to the other side of the city. The girls at school loved the music we put together. That was all I needed. We came up with another brilliant idea.

Instead of going to the grade 7 dance, we would DJ our own house party. We knew we could sneak some drinks in, and we'd be able to dance up on the girls however we wanted to without Mrs. Mitchell smacking us in the ass with a metre stick, telling the girls, "Keep your booties off the boys!"

Music is the voice of the poor people. It's the sound of the Caribbean. It breaks boundaries and brings people together. West Indian people are all about community. If all the kids wanted to come out to a party in your basement, at least you knew they were safe. You could keep an eye on them, and for once, knew they weren't getting into some real trouble. Moms would come down with nuts and snacks. I remember one who had *the* best punch — it made you feel like you were drinking on a beach in Guyana. She didn't know we were pouring vodka in it when she went back upstairs. Dads would play security and caretaker, making sure nobody really destroyed the place. "Stop bangin' on de damn furnace!"

Our parties were the hottest thing around, like a Sean Paul music video. That's where Director X got the idea for "Get Busy." He grew up at parties like ours. Everybody in Scarborough wanted to come out to our parties. Most of the time, there were more high school kids in the jam than middle schoolers. That's probably how we were always able to keep the good liquor around. Red Flame, Roots Royalty, Lindo P, and DJ Shamann would spin our parties. These guys were playing at nightclubs downtown, but our parties were so hot they would DJ them for us!

All good things come to an end. Our last party at the end of grade 8 had to be the baddest one that would have everybody talking about it forever. The parents were all on board because they knew after this, we would be off doing our own thing, making far worse choices. But they didn't have a clue how big our ideas were.

Spectrum was the big club on Danforth Avenue, but it was empty that night because their best DJs were working our party. That took our status through the roof. Everybody wanted to come out to this last party.

If you could have fit a hundred people in that basement, we had two hundred in there. It was so rammed, you could barely move. But there wasn't a person in there who wanted to leave. My friend's dad called me upstairs, "DeRo, yuh brother outside! Ya hav fe come now!" I opened the door and there were two hundred people on the front lawn.

It didn't last much longer after that. There wasn't a person on that block who would have called the cops, but the police know what it sounds like when something big is going down in Scarborough. The quickest way to thin out a crowd is to have a Toronto police cruiser with the lights on roll down the street. They don't even need to put the sirens on.

CHAPTER 2

CHOICES

The older we got, the more shit we got up to. Stealing cars was a big thing in high school. I never did it, because I didn't need to. My dude would roll up in something new every Friday night: sometimes it would be a Plymouth, other times he'd swipe a Caravan so we could put eight or nine of the boys in there. They weren't the hottest cars. But they were the easiest for the boys to break into.

It was always just a joy ride. We didn't know there was an international network of car thieves and money to be made. There probably weren't too many 15-year-old Toyota Corollas or Acura Integras being loaded onto those cargo ships anyway. We just wanted to get places.

We'd roll up to the clubs in those cars, hollering at girls that were probably 5 or 10 years older than us. Maybe we didn't look as cool as we thought sliding open the minivan door, but we felt cool as hell. We were only 14 or 15 years old.

Imagine being a 20-year-old standing in line at the club with your girlfriend, and these kids roll out of a soccer mom van trying to impress her. We were crazy. I still don't know how we actually got in the club, but there was always somebody willing to look the other way and let us do what we wanted. Scarborough is a different kind of place.

I'll never forget the last joyride. We were driving up Kennedy Road at 2 a.m. one night, when a police cruiser passed us. All of a sudden, we were the only two cars on the road. You could actually feel everyone hold their breath. The cop made a hard U-turn and threw the sirens on. "Oh shit, what the hell do we do?"

The car was stolen. Nobody had a license. I knew my Auntie wouldn't pick me up from jail. That fight-or-flight response kicked in, and for the first time, it wasn't fight.

I opened up the sliding door and jumped out of the van. I hit the pavement so hard, I thought I had broken my neck.

The van was probably going 60 km/h. We didn't stand a chance racing a police-tuned Ford Crown Victoria. The car chase was over in about five seconds, and all five guys jumped out and ran away. That was my chance. I picked myself up off the road and ran straight towards the first backyard I saw. I've never jumped a fence so easily while in so much pain.

Before I got across the yard, I heard a policeman yelling at me and could see his flashlight. No need for Advil. That pain was gone. I was hurdling fences like an Olympian. But so was the cop. I probably jumped through 10 backyards before I reached the train tracks. I cleared the last fence and landed right in a thorn bush.

I hadn't realized the cop had stopped trailing me. Sirens were blaring in the distance, but police cars couldn't drive down the train tracks so I waited out of sight in the thorn bush until I couldn't take it anymore.

The streets weren't safe, so I hopped backyards again. Jump a fence, deal with a barking dog, hop another, deal with another dog. Jump one more, hope the policeman wasn't waiting for me. I did that for seven kilometres, all the way to Lawrence East Station. I had never been more exhausted in my life. And I still had to take a bus home, with my shirt all cut up and my arms bleeding everywhere. I don't know how the bus driver let me on.

Nobody got caught that night. Every single one of us got away. We couldn't believe it when we all showed up at school the next morning and the cops never came to take us away before the final bell.

I had jumped out of a moving van, hurdled fences in complete darkness to outrun a cop, got stuck in a damn thorn bush, backyard-hopped my way home, and lived to tell the tale. I took this as a sign — I never rode in a stolen car again.

Every time I did something bad, I knew my dad would be pissed. But I didn't want to let my Aunt down — she had given up her life to raise us. So I always felt bad every time I did some dumb shit. When we got pinched for stealing VCRs at school, I couldn't look her in the eye. We were playing basketball at some fancy prep school, and I spotted the TV trolley in one of the classrooms. The door to the room was locked, so we went outside and cracked the window open. We couldn't get the TV through, so we just stole the VCR. The police showed up at our front door the next day. They had caught everything on camera. We didn't even know they had cameras; we were that young.

———

As bad as we were, we were good guys. And I'm not just talking about Boys in Blue, but all the crews. These boys had good souls. We were just kids who didn't know what to do with ourselves. We were frustrated with life. It was harder to stay out of trouble than it was to find it.

If I hadn't fallen in love with sports as a kid, I'd probably be in prison right now. A lot of us would have been in jail way before we turned 18.

Playing sports was always a constant in my life. I could have been a great badminton player. I had a killer game in elementary school. I would thrash that birdie like it insulted my Auntie. But the Asians killed me: they'd lure me in, then find the corners. I couldn't win anymore. That killed it for me. And what was I gonna say? "Yo, bredren. Let's go play badminton." Nobody was doing that.

There was a ball at my feet from the time I was able to walk. A lot of times, it wasn't even a soccer ball. We would roll up a bunch of socks into a ball and kick it around the apartment. Chair legs made the best goal posts. There wasn't much room for error, so your touch had to be perfect.

Maybe that's where I really perfected my shot accuracy. Those games were intense; we were always so competitive all the time.

I'd play basketball with my brothers and with the crew all the time. We had our own community teams and would play at the gym or a schoolyard court whenever we wanted.

I almost chose basketball.

Nobody could catch me running up the court, and because I was small it was easy to weave through kids and get to the hoop. I played point guard and ran the offense for the Toronto Blues provincial team. We won the bantam championship. We won the junior championship. Everybody thinks basketball got big in Canada after Vince Carter, but we were good back then. Those kids could ball hard. Playing against older kids in the hood all the time, especially my brothers, I could read the game so much better and faster than any of the kids my age. It didn't matter how tall the kid was guarding me. I had this high arching shot that I could shoot from anywhere. The taller the defender, the more likely I was to try the difficult shot just so I could see the stupid look on his face. I loved that feeling. I still love it.

And I felt like basketball was *my* thing. My brothers were older, so they weren't on the same competitive teams as me by the time I was in high school. And unlike in soccer, my dad wasn't my coach.

My dad always wanted the best for me when he was my soccer coach. But, of course, he treated me differently than he did the other kids, and that eventually got to me. At 14, I thought I knew everything already anyway. I was a star player in two sports. I was hustling in the neighbourhood. Girls loved me. I felt like the king of Scarborough. I wasn't going to listen to anyone who yelled at me. And nobody yelled like my dad. At basketball, I didn't have that. I had more control to influence the game than when I played with 10 other kids on a soccer field. There was more freedom to be the star.

Every kid who grows up playing multiple sports has to make a choice at some point. There comes a time where you have to fully commit 100 percent to one or the other. There just isn't enough time in the day to do all you need to do to keep developing to reach the next level.

Soccer was my first love. It had already given me a world of opportunities. I played in my first overseas tournament at the age of 10: The Canary Cup, in Swansea, Wales.

The head coach of London Youth Soccer (in London, Ontario), Ted Nezic, was so impressed by me after my team, the Malvern Magic, played their team. He called my dad, who was our coach, and asked if I could train with his team ahead of their trip to Britain. That was a lot to ask. But my dad always supported me, and he knew this could be a great opportunity, so he drove me down to London for a few weekends so I could play with Ted's team. Sometimes I would sleep over at Ted's house, and Ted would make the two-hour drive back to Scarborough so I could go to school on Monday. Ted wanted me to play for his team so bad, they organized a couple of fundraisers to raise the money to fly me, my dad, his girlfriend and her son, my Auntie, and my two brothers to Wales, just so I could play in this tournament.

It was the trip of a lifetime. We'd never been on a plane before. All I knew was Kennedy and Eglinton in Scarborough. I remember feeling like we were going to be on that giant-ass plane forever. What a different world when we stepped off it. Cars driving on the wrong side of the road. Buildings that were hundreds of years old. Fish and chips all the time. My only exposure to Great Britain before then was what I saw on TV, on Soccer Saturday with Graham Leggat. They put us all up in a three-bedroom house and gave us a car so we could get around. If we weren't at the house or at the field, we were visiting some castle. I'd never seen anything like them. My whole block could live in some of them. My brothers and I played soccer in that basement every day. There were a lot of dents in the wall by the time we left.

Most of the kids on my team had only travelled as far as Quebec and neighbouring American states before. The tournament was such a learning experience for all of us. We played against kids from England and Scotland and from a couple other European countries. We did well. If they had one advantage, it was that they knew how to play in that British weather. Damn it was cold. I think it rained every single game we played and I was cold for the full 90 minutes. At least the grass was great. We must have beat it up, but I remember it being so clean and so green. We didn't have any fields like that in Scarborough.

Soccer was taking me places. By 14, I had played all over the United States, in Europe, and even in South America. Soccer is the world's game, and now it was taking me around the world. Not everybody thought the world of me though.

I'll never forget the look on my dad's face when I got cut from Canada's U-17 team before the 1993 U-17 World Cup in Japan. Bob Monroe was my coach and he called the two of us into his office after some big exhausting tournament. "I'll just get straight to the point. Dwayne has all the skill in the world. But he's too small, so we're going to let him go from the program."

I was stunned. What he was saying didn't make any sense to me. How could you compliment me for being so skilled but cut me because I was too small? I was a teenager! I wasn't done growing. At that age, height is never the most important thing.

My dad was more pissed than I was — probably because he was the one driving me around every weekend, and now it felt like a waste. It wasn't. Getting cut was the fuel I needed to keep going and to work harder.

In my mind, I wanted to change Canada Soccer. I didn't only want to change it for me. There were a lot of kids that didn't make it because of their philosophy of teaching and what they were looking for in players. Dump and chase. Beat your opposition with your physicality. A lot of us didn't embrace that. We wanted to beat Mexico and these Central American teams at their own game. When I was a kid, U.S. Soccer was nothing. I played on teams that went down there and won tournaments all the time. But when I played with the Canadian national program, there was this disconnect. We only wanted to beat them physically. We didn't want to beat the Americans at soccer. Over the years, the more we focused on beating them down, the stronger they got. The faster they got. The better they got on the ball. Their confidence level was so much higher than ours. And look at the World Cup success they've had over the last 20 years.

I knew I wasn't too small for Bob's team. Before him, Barry Maclean was my coach at the provincial level and he had our team play men's league teams all the time, like Toronto Croatia. It was difficult. It was physical. We used to get in fights and knock people out. I was nearly taken to court for assault one time. This guy was hacking me and hacking me, all game. When you're a good player, you just expect that, but this guy was relentless. Finally I'd had enough. He tripped me up on the edge of the 18-yard box. It was a dirty tackle.

He stood over me, yelling, "Stop diving for a call. You're outside the box! Get the fuck up kid!"

I shot right up and cracked him in the jaw with a left hook. He dropped like a pancake. I'm right-handed — I didn't know how strong I was with my left hand. His team was raging mad. Their biggest guy charged at me. I didn't know what I was going to do, but luckily, I didn't have to do anything. My friend Kashka Walker came flying in and karate kicked him in the chest. It was like one of those grainy videos you see on YouTube, where you're left wondering, "Damn! What country is that in?"

———

It was special when I first started playing in the national program. The red and white draped over my skin. That maple leaf on top of my heart. Now I was getting paid to play soccer. A lot of my friends' parents didn't have jobs, and here I was, a carded athlete, which meant I was approved for funding and was getting paid by the government to play in the national soccer program. What a life.

It wasn't lost on me how much harder it was for the people around me. I was 14 years old, with multiple sources of income. So I shared it. I started chipping in on the rent. I would do all the grocery shopping one week. Whatever my family wanted, they could take.

My dad never asked for anything. He was a proud Caribbean man who worked hard for absolutely everything he had. Providing for his sons was his main drive in life. If he couldn't get something he needed, he went without. But my dad always made sure we never did.

So when things were really bad, Auntie Lea would ask me for help. When Dad's car broke down, he couldn't afford the repairs along with everything else. That car was the most valuable possession he had. Without it, he couldn't get to work, bring me to soccer practice, or take my brothers where they needed to go. He would've done anything to be able to provide for us no matter how dangerous or how demanding. But he would never ask me for help. My aunt knew that.

That's why she asked me. I was proud to be able to provide. For the first time in my life, I had a real purpose now. I wasn't just a kid wasting time on the streets, getting up to trouble. The people I depended on for so long could now turn to me if and when they needed to. Not even my brothers knew I was doing that.

I started to look at the whole picture. All around me, things were changing. The block didn't look the same anymore. Some of the people I rolled with had moved away. Some of them were in jail. Everybody was growing up. I hadn't even finished grade 10, and I was living three separate lives.

There was "Iman DeRo."

I knew where to get the best herb, and I made the best mix tapes. If you didn't want one, you wanted the other.

There was "Soccer DeRo."

I was playing at really competitive levels now. Teams and coaches knew how much talent I had, and everyone else knew I was a hard worker. What they didn't know was that I would be out with my crew at a club until 4 a.m., then get up at 5 a.m. to go out to Hamilton to train with the provincial team, then I'd come back to the city to play indoor soccer with my regular team or play a league game. I would do that every Saturday and Sunday. And then again every Tuesday and Thursday. It was an insane cycle. They didn't know I could've been out selling weed or getting into fights the night before. I'd be home by morning and ready to trek out and train with these guys. None of these kids grew up the way I did, so I had a new group to run with. They saw the world differently and didn't know anything about the trouble I got up to in the neighbourhood. They saw me in a different way than everybody else I knew.

And then there was "Home DeRo."

Where I come from, you gotta grow up quick. I felt lucky to be able to chip in to keep the household running. I was beginning to see how much more I had to offer. I knew I had to make a choice.

Did I want to be the richest drug dealer around? Or did I want to be the best soccer player in the world?

I'm Canadian, so you might think both of those ideas are ludicrous. Not to me. I knew whatever I committed to 100 percent, I would achieve. I didn't know the path to reach the top of the soccer world, but I believed I could get there. I did know what I had to do if I chose the other option.

To become Scarborough's Pablo Escobar, I would have to take the hustle to new levels and start doing things I really did not want to do.

If you sold weed, you always had money. Cash would literally burn a hole in the baggy ass pockets of anyone who pushed it. But if you wanted to get rich, you sold crack. Everybody talks about crack in America in the 1980s. Nobody seemed to notice what it was doing to my community. I sure did.

The first time someone offered me crack to sell, I knew I wouldn't. It didn't matter how much money I could've made. If you told me, "Sell this little bit of crack and you'll make $100,000," I still wouldn't have done it. I saw what crack was doing to the mothers in my neighbourhood. It was awful. There was no way I was going to make money off of the poison that was literally destroying my community and the families I knew and cared about.

There were a lot of ways to make money — not just through the drug trade. A lot of my friends were robbing gas stations and convenience stores. Some guys were actually robbing banks. Dealing was too much work; robbing was a whole lot easier. But I didn't want to do that. I didn't want that life and I wasn't going to hurt someone to get ahead.

I was at a crossroads. Living three lives was exhausting. It seemed like every day started the same way, with dad yelling at me: "Dwayne! Get up! Time to go."

Oh man, here we go again. Change. Eat. Get in the car and drive to soccer. On the way there, I hated it. I didn't have any energy. I wouldn't admit that to anybody though. It was easier to complain about something else. "It's cold. I don't know how I can keep doing this." My dad never had any time for that one. He could complain about the weather, but I couldn't.

I would watch as kids I played with growing up quit one by one. Good kids from Scarborough who had all the skill and all the ability would eventually just give up. Like me, some of them were trying to balance all of these opportunities and getting up to all the trouble I was. No one can live like that forever. I couldn't. But I wouldn't quit.

To this day, a lot of people don't know what I got up to growing up. I knew what I was doing was wrong, so I didn't want anybody to know. That made me a very private person. Only one or two kids knew what I was getting up to on the streets. I didn't want any of the players or coaches to know. I didn't want my brothers to know. My business was my business.

Like all big life decisions, you toy with it and go back and forth until something happens . . . and then one day you just know what to do.

CHAPTER 3

GUN TO MY HEAD

Having a big crew means you always have somewhere to hang out. I couldn't have parties or people over at our apartment, so I spent a lot of time hanging out in my friends' basements, eating their mother's sweet cooking.

One day I went over to my buddy's house and another friend of his from a different school was over. Let's call him James. I didn't know James, but he seemed cool. Any friend of my boy was cool with me.

We hung out in the basement for hours just listening to music, talking about girls, and probably planning more trouble with another crew. I could tell James didn't roll with guys like us. There was just something funny about this kid that I spotted early on.

At some point my friend went upstairs and James turned to me with this strange grin on his face.

"Yo, DeRo, I want to show you something."

He reached into his school bag and pulled out a gun.

Very impressed with his show-and-tell piece, James was shocked that I wasn't.

"What the fuck are you gonna do with that?" I asked him.

Real tough guys didn't carry guns. Nobody in my crew had a gun, and none of the guys we scrapped with did either. So who the hell did this guy think he was?

Clearly James didn't think the same way as me. Having a piece made him feel like a real gangster, like someone who couldn't be messed with. I thought he was a bitch and told him that as he swung it around, showing off like he knew what he was doing with a 9 mm in his hand.

He thought he was so cool with his new toy. I don't know where he got it from or how long he'd had it for, but he looked like an idiot with it.

"I'll shoot anybody that looks at me funny," he joked.

I'd had enough of this kid by now. James was a loser who I would never hang out with outside of my buddy's basement.

"You wouldn't shoot anybody, man. You're a bitch."

I stood up to go upstairs. I knew my friend would react the exact same way to this punk. Fake tough guys were a waste of my time, and I told James that's all he was. He didn't like that.

He stood up and walked towards me. James was probably six inches taller than me, but that didn't intimidate me at all and I laughed at him as he squared up to me. I could see in his face that my attitude was really starting to piss him off.

"I ain't scared of no tall kid with a fake gun!"

I wasn't scared of anybody. He looked down at the gun in his hand and started chuckling to himself.

"You're a bitch!" I said again. He was mad now.

He looked up at me and pointed the gun to my head.

I laughed at him. He was testing me. There was no way he was going to shoot me in our friend's basement. I wasn't afraid, but I could feel the weight of the cold gun against my forehead.

"Call me a 'bitch' again, and I'm gonna pull the trigger!"

When you're that age, you don't fear death. I was more afraid he thought he could bully me and get away with it.

How crazy is that? With a gun pointed at my head, I was actually more worried that he would think I was weak. So of course I said it again, "Bro, you're a bitch!"

Bang.

He pulled the trigger and shot me right in the eye. Fuck.

I didn't fall. I was in shock. He shot me. How was I still standing? The pain was incredible. I pulled my hands up to my face. They were covered in blood. I scrambled to the bathroom a few feet away. I was still trying to process what had happened. How was I not lying on the floor dead? How was I able to run to the bathroom and look at myself in the mirror?

All I could see was blood. It was like I was wearing a red eye patch. I couldn't see anything out of that eye. Rage washed over me. I wanted to kill that motherfucker. I grabbed a bowl that was on the side of the bathroom sink and stormed out after him. He was gone. My friend could hear me screaming and came scrambling through the kitchen as I sprinted up the stairs.

"DeRo! What the hell happened?"

"Your boy just shot me! Where the fuck is he?"

"What? What do you mean, he shot you? How the hell are you standing right now?'

I couldn't answer that question. I didn't know, and I didn't care. All I cared about was finding this kid so I could make him pay. But I was in bad shape. My friend convinced me to chill and take care of my eye. We must have ruined a dozen of his mom's towels. Eventually my eye stopped bleeding and I could start to see just a little bit. It wasn't as dark red anymore, and I wasn't as enraged. I realized how lucky I was.

He didn't shoot me with a bullet. I don't know if he couldn't get any or if he was just too cheap to buy them, but he had packed the chamber with dirt and small nails. It did some real damage. But I was alive.

The most important thing now was: don't let Dad find out.

It's crazy that after that trauma, in all that panic, all I could think was, "Dad's gonna kill me if he knew I was hanging around guns. *And then he'd go after James.*"

I was able to see well enough to leave my buddy's house and walk home. Every hour, I could see a little bit more out of my eye. I thought I would be just fine eventually. I needed to be. My team, G.S. United, was playing a tournament that weekend at the SkyDome. It would be my first time playing in a 50,000-seat stadium. I couldn't miss that.

My brothers were there when I got home and knew something was up. I wasn't bleeding anymore, but my eye was messed. They couldn't believe what had happened. They couldn't believe how lucky I was. Naturally, they wanted to rush out of there and make that kid pay. I told them they couldn't. They at least had to wait and help me avoid Auntie and Dad in the apartment. Not easy to do. But I somehow made it to the tournament two days later with my dad probably thinking I was weird for wearing sunglasses indoors.

Uncle Dave Sidhu was the coach and Dad was his assistant. Uncle Dave noticed my eye was red just before the game kicked off. I told him I had been poked in the eye during warm-up. Running around in the game, my eye started to fill up with blood again. It was bad. I probably had just 30 percent of my vision when we got there, but now I couldn't see anything out of that eye.

I was scared now. I told my dad I had to come out of the game. We got in the car and drove straight to an eye doctor.

"You ready to tell me what really happened now?"

My eye had looked bad for two days. My dad must have noticed but just hadn't said anything. I doubled down on the lie, saying I got poked with a finger and then the bad air in the stadium made it worse.

When we got to the eye doctor, the red flags really went up.

"This is serious. You've got to take him to St. Mike's hospital right now. Dwayne might have a complete retinal detachment."

Back in the car we went. Now my dad was angry. I had to tell him the whole truth. He was shocked.

"Do you know how stupid you are for playing around with guns? You could be blind right now! Soccer over. Living life like a blind man. You don't know how lucky you are to still have your sight!"

I had torn my retina. There was a cut on the edge of my eye socket where a nail must have hit. The doctor said, "You're a lucky guy. If the nail had been a millimetre to the left, you would have lost your eye, son."

I didn't need him to tell me that. I may not have been smart enough to go to the hospital right away, but I knew I was lucky to be alive.

The recovery process was serious. I had to get laser surgery and was going to the clinic and getting tested for almost two years. It really felt like it was never going to end. It probably should've derailed my soccer career right then and there. The doctors wouldn't allow me to play because I had to keep my head free from contact. Of course, I was a knucklehead kid so I didn't listen. After a couple of months, I told my dad I was fine and got the okay from the doctors to get back on the field. I should've taken more time.

That trauma affected me for the rest of my life. For the last three to four years of my career, I couldn't see properly out of that eye. I was pretty much a one-eyed man out there on the field. I played with a lot of floaters that would get in the way of my vision. If you watch my old games, you can see me rubbing my eye all the time because in the moment I thought I had dust or something in my eye. Those really sunny days were the worst.

Nobody knew what I was dealing with. Once I turned 30, my eye got worse every year. I used to cheat my way through the eye exams: I'd spot the letters with my good eye and then cover up and pretend I was reading them clean with my bad one. Then I'd chat the docs up and distract them so I could dash out of there. Those were some of the most stressful days of my life.

I didn't seek the right help while I was playing because I didn't want to jeopardize my career. No coach would have cared as long as I was performing. But if I had slipped up, that would have been the easiest excuse to bench me or rip up my contract. It was dangerous to wait until I retired to get it treated, but I wouldn't have been able to recover or receive the right treatment while playing at the top level.

The worse it got, the more my game had to adapt. I had to check my shoulders more than I normally would because I wouldn't be able to see the defenders. If I glanced to my left, I couldn't really see where the space was or where the defender was. So I would use my hands a lot and turn my whole head just so I could see. When I started playing on the left side for Canada, it was a real challenge. The defender was coming in on my blind side, literally. Every time I got the ball, I would take it a touch inside so I could square up and see the whole field properly with my good eye. There were subtle things I had to do to adjust to the play, and that just became normal for me. I don't think anybody had any idea.

I like to think I was a player who always played with all my senses — someone who could feel where the player was instead of seeing exactly where he was. Making the right pass is all about timing. Like when a player made a run and I'd backheel it to him, I couldn't see the man. But I could feel the weight of his heels hitting the ground and the pace he was running at. If you're able to take all that in, then you can place it perfectly for them. Obviously, I couldn't just rely on my vision, so my game was all about feeling.

That near death experience was the moment I needed to change my life for good. That's when it hit me. I was done.

I had to get away from that street life. I knew if I didn't, it wasn't going to end well for anybody. All I had to do was count the number of people who weren't in my life anymore because they were in jail or because they had to leave the hood. I'd heard of so many people that were serving hard time, or were killed before the age of 25. I'd think, "Damn, I knew who he was. Sorry for his family." Then I'd move on. But move on to what? It was a never-ending train to nowhere.

I started to wake up and realize I had so much more to live for than that shit.

I had my family. I had soccer. I didn't need the streets. Dwayne De Rosario wasn't going to be another statistic. I made the choice: soccer would be my life.

CHAPTER 4

SCARBOROUGH TO THE WORLD

Like any other business, soccer is about connections. And let's just get this out of the way now: even at the youth level, soccer is very much a business. There's so much money at the top, and that's what drives and dictates everything below. Connections lead to opportunity, and sometimes they come from the most surprising places. You meet so many people in the sport, you never know when, where, or why your paths may cross again.

My dad's girlfriend, Rose, was Italian and had a connection with Toronto Azzurri Soccer club. Like my opportunity with Ted and his London Youth Soccer team, they were planning an overseas trip and wanted me to join them. But they were heading to Turin, Italy, home to one of the greatest clubs in the world, Juventus F.C.

The only thing this trip had in common with our big Welsh adventure was that I flew on a plane to get there. Everything else about this trip was different. The weather was better, and there were more kids on the team who read the game the way I did and played with a bit more flare. I was older now and didn't have the whole family entourage with me, so I could room with my fellow players. We went out on the town every night. It was my first time seeing Venice, Rome, and all these picturesque places I had only seen in books or on TV. Italy is even more beautiful in person. So is the soccer.

Italian soccer is so much more tactical than what I experienced in that Wales tournament. I was more prepared for Italian football than British-style football. Even now I don't enjoy that dump and run football. We played Parma, Fiorentina, and a couple of other clubs — all quality teams. It was a real test for all of us.

After the last game, this English gentleman who was somehow affiliated with the tournament invited me to trial with Portsmouth F.C., in England. Nothing happened at the time, and we all went back to Canada. The next year Toronto Azzurri went to England for another showcase tournament. Except it wasn't the same youth tournament — we were playing against grown men. It was all about football now. We weren't going out; we weren't staying up late. We did well against these men's teams. The tournament finished and everyone flew home, except me.

My dad reached out to that English agent we had met in Italy. He came through on his promise. I went down to Portsmouth to train at Pompey for two weeks. It had been arranged that I billet with a family that was housing another Canadian kid from Vancouver. Normally, I love being with Canadians, but he was younger than me, and I didn't like that I was staying with a younger kid. And I didn't like that I was staying with a family I didn't know. The billet lady was nice, but I didn't like the food she was cooking, so I would sneak out after dinner and find Indian food in town. I returned to Canada, knowing this wasn't the right place for me.

It was becoming clear that so many people wanted to invest in me. Someone wanted me here, someone wanted me there. If the flight was taken care of, I went. I didn't know what would happen when it came to the soccer, but it was a great way to see the world. I was seeing places no one in my community was seeing. I'd been to South America, France, all over the U.S., the Caribbean — and on someone else's dime. Today, it's different. Now these parents are baited into paying a fortune for camps and tryouts in the hopes that their kid *might* make it.

I realized pretty quickly that these people bringing me around the world to different professional organizations had their own agendas. The people introducing me to the clubs were looking for a finder's fee. I didn't have any professional representation. Not many Canadian kids were getting looks from European teams. That made me very appealing to anyone who was looking to build their own career and line their own pockets in the process.

These people were acting as my handlers. I wasn't involved in their discussions with the clubs. I was just given a plane ticket, put up somewhere, dropped off at a certain time, and told to play my game. These people could have asked for $1 million, and if the club balked, they would just take me away. And without having any say, I would lose my chance with that team. I really will never know how many times that may have happened.

———

I was happy to take advantage of the free trips. I didn't mind travelling. I'd fly off, spend a few days with a team, fly back. Nothing would happen. Okay, when's the next one? It was a challenge for me, and I was getting to see the world: Marseille, Tel Aviv, Sweden, Beijing. I'd go out and explore to try to make the most of being there. Few places really pulled me; most just made me curious for the next trip. I remember thinking, "Maybe I could live in Budapest." MTK Budapest is the biggest club in Hungary, and when they brought me over on trial I thought it might actually lead to something. It didn't, and I'll never know why.

I needed to be more selective with my trials. I was becoming more and more confident in my game and felt like something bigger was just around the corner.

A.C. Milan were the kings of Italian soccer in the 1990s. They won five league titles and two European Cups in that decade. It didn't matter where you were in the world, when you saw red and black stripes, you knew it was A.C. Milan.

Boarding the flight from Toronto to Milan felt different. Everything about the journey was. The airline staff was dressed nicer, as were all the passengers on board. The seats were bigger. They served real food on the flight. Even my name sounded Italian when the flight attendant welcomed me on, "Buon viaggio, Signore De Rosario." There weren't many kids who looked like me on these flights. The man who sat next to me asked, "What brings you to Italy all by yourself?"

"I'm going to try out for A.C. Milan."

It didn't even sound real when I said it out loud.

"Wow. Congratulations, young man. The San Siro is a cathedral of football," he said.

I had never heard anyone describe a soccer stadium like that before. He wasn't lying. Some of the best players in the world have kicked a ball on that field. Eighty thousand people show up every weekend to watch A.C. Milan or their local rivals, Inter Milan.

I walked through life as a confident kid with my nose in the air. But when I stepped onto that green grass for the first time, wearing an A.C. Milan badge on my shirt, I looked down and couldn't take my eyes off the ground. My steps felt slow, but the training sessions were anything but. A lot of great players have come through that academy. It's a system that weeds out the weak. By that age, most of the kids I was playing with had played together for years. Some had played together for half their lives. Everything was quick: your touch had to be quick, and your decision-making had to be quicker. You were expected to read the game like it was a book you had memorized. It was very regimented.

After a couple of days, I finally got to see what we had been working on in those sessions perfected. A.C. Milan played a cup match. I sat in a suite with some academy players and coaches. Many of them were excited to practice their English because I was there. I don't think I said a word to anybody. I couldn't take my eyes off the game. It wasn't soccer. It was art.

I was sitting in one of the most historic stadiums in the world, watching some of the best players in the world. Paolo Maldini. Marcel Desailly. Edgar Davids. Roberto Baggio. George Weah. I didn't want that match to end. I could've stayed in that seat forever.

George Weah is one of the best players I have ever seen play in person. He could run at full speed and dribble the ball like he was walking.

Nobody could stop him. When people talk about the greatest players of all time, he often gets forgotten because he never played in a World Cup. He is the only African player to ever win the FIFA Ballon d'Or. For me, George Weah is on the podium with Pelé and Diego Maradona. And if he was English or French, the world would put him there too.

The next day, some of the A.C. Milan players were in the locker room when we showed up for our session. After a big match, there's always a few players who need the trainer's table in the morning. I knew it was going to be one of my last sessions, so I felt lucky to meet a few of the guys. Edgar Davids was standing there, looking like a guy I could run into at Scarborough Town Centre. His dreadlocks weren't very long at the time, and he wasn't wearing glasses yet. A.C. Milan had a history of signing super-talented Dutch players. He was the latest one. I introduced myself and told him I had watched the game the night before. Surprisingly, he knew who I was before I said anything.

"You're that Canadian kid. What are you doing over here? You're not gonna make it here, kid. This is not a place for Canadians."

His nickname was "The Pitbull." And man, did that ever bite. Why would he say that to me? Was he right? He hadn't even seen me play. I couldn't get those words out of my head for the rest of the day. I don't think I heard one coaching instruction in that training session. The only voice I could hear was the one in my head, repeating, "You're Canadian. You don't belong here."

Little did I know, that was an opinion a lot of people shared. Not just in Italy, or amongst Dutch people. Most of the world thought that way, and still does. At that time, Canadian-born players were just starting to get opportunities to play in Europe. There were no stars. There was no one who could hold their own in a lineup of those players I watched at the San Siro. Not yet.

And although the final session was my worst session by far, it didn't matter. A.C. Milan offered me a five-year contract.

Five years. At A.C. Milan. Wow.

Five years is a long time for a 17-year-old. Five years seemed like the rest of my life. It was a contract I couldn't sign. Not for five years, with no guarantee that I would get to play on the first team or get the chance to kick Edgar Davids in training.

I turned it down. I called my dad and told him it wasn't what I wanted. "Okay, Dwayne. Come home, son."

I don't call it a regret — I truly don't like to use that word. Of course there are things I look back on and wonder, "What if?" This is one of them. But I don't regret turning the opportunity down. I can look back now and accept that I just wasn't ready. Davids was wrong. I knew I could play. I knew it would've been a great environment to develop my game. But I didn't know how to be the person who could succeed in that place. Train at this time, eat at this time, sleep at this time. Repeat. I didn't want to put that work in. Not because I was lazy — I definitely knew I was good enough to be there and could hold my own — I just wasn't ready to move halfway across the world and be apart from my family.

Back home I had my people. I was enjoying playing with G.S. United in Scarborough. I was playing regularly with the provincial team and people were always telling me, "Don't worry about Europe, DeRo. You're going places. You're going to play for Canada one day." But there weren't many coaches in the national set-up who wanted to play the game like I did.

Most countries have their own identity when it comes to soccer — something that has been developed and refined for decades. Canadian soccer's DNA has a very strong British influence: run, dump, beat down and batter the other team, and force your way to win. It's the Bob Lenarduzzi style that Canada played to reach the World Cup in 1986, our one and only World Cup appearance.

I hated that soccer. My dad raised us with Brazilian ideals. Play from the back. Play with flare. Express yourself and enjoy the game. Keep the ball on the carpet, and if there's a problem, solve it, don't just dump it down.

I played for so many negative coaches. Their solution to everything was, "JUST GET IT UP THE FIELD! LUMP IT! LUMP IT FORWARD!" Not every English, Scottish, and Irish coach was like that, but all the ones I'm thinking about were. They didn't see the game the way Caribbeans, Latinos, Portuguese, or Italians did. Shield a man, control it, play it back to the keeper. Keep possession. We had ballers in the national program that understood that, but we had to change our style to suit the coaches because they didn't want to play that way. Look at the game now; kick-and-run soccer just doesn't work anymore. But that's what we did.

The only coach who really embraced my game, outside of my coaches from Scarborough that is, was Bruce Twamley.

Bruce was my saviour. He was a saviour for a lot of us. He understood the kick-and-run style that he was expected to play, but he also understood me. He liked guys who were edgy. The program wanted every team to play a 3-5-1 formation, with a dump, chase, and pray philosophy. Bruce wanted to play with the players he had in front of him. A good coach plays with the tools he has; a great coach knows how to use them.

"DeRo, you got something special, and I want you to keep that. Keep taking guys on. Be who you are out there."

We got on really well. I stayed at his house with his family, and he took me in as one of his own. If it wasn't for Bruce, I probably would've quit soccer.

Bruce was the coach of Team Canada at the 1997 FIFA World Youth Championship (now the FIFA U-20 World Cup) in Malaysia. Before getting there, we dominated a qualifying tournament in Mexico. We were playing proper soccer, and we had more passion and heart than anybody else out there. Bruce got us to rally around the cause. He understood us, and he knew we were hungry. He knew how to crack the whip, and he knew when to step back and let us be us, especially me. If you crack the whip too much on me, I might pick it up and crack it back on you, even if it cost me. When Bruce would pull me aside, it was either, "DeRo, you're fucking driving me crazy!" or "DeRo, that was amazing!"

I thought Bruce was going to be the next national team coach. Players loved playing for him. He didn't care what your deal was or where you were from. He didn't care if you were purple. If you could play, Bruce gave you a chance on his team. He fought for us to get trip sponsorships and was a very progressive thinker. But Canada Soccer thought he was *too* unconventional.

Bruce is one of those guys who did so much for the game in this country, and few people know it. He got boxed out of the national team program because he didn't take people's shit. Bruce wasn't a conformist. I know in my heart if Bruce Twamley was given the national team job permanently, Canada would have played in a World Cup.

Before that qualifying tournament in Mexico, Bruce took me on trial to FC Barcelona. Bobby Robson was the manager at the time, and somehow Bruce had a connection. I was at home, arguing about something stupid with my brothers, when Bruce called.

"I've got the opportunity of a lifetime for you. I've got a contact who can get you a trial with Barcelona's youth team."

My first thought wasn't "Could this be my chance?" or "Will this be any different than A.C. Milan?" It was simpler. I didn't have the money to just pack up and fly out to Barcelona. I don't know how, but Bruce got me over there.

It was 1996, just after Barcelona bought Ronaldo from PSV Eindhoven in the Netherlands for a record $19.5 million. I could barely wrap my head around that. Ronaldo was barely two years older than me, and they had labelled him "the future of Barcelona." Everyone at La Masia was buzzing about the signing. All I could think was, "Yeah, okay, he's a great player. Just watch me when I come on."

I was training at the best academy in the world. The entire place ran like a well-oiled machine. Every day, the kit man laid out the change room like we were a professional team. The grass was cut at the same time every day. The cooks prepared our meals at the same time every day. Just like the Barcelona philosophy, everything was done with a purpose. It's no secret why they've been able to produce so many world-class players.

We played a game at the youth stadium. This was my audition, and I was ready to steal the show. I won every 50-50 ball, handled every pass, did everything right. I impressed myself, and I impressed Barca. They really liked my game, but I probably should've expected their verdict:

"Listen, we've pretty much invested so much in signing Ronaldo, we can't sign any more players."

Just my luck. They did offer me a per diem to train at La Masia, but they couldn't sign me to a real contract.

Before I left, I got to see Ronaldo play against Valencia. I was sitting five rows up with the youth team. I was taken aback. This guy was amazing. He was the only player who stood out on the pitch. Effortless individualism. His touch on the ball, the way he would drop his shoulders and shift side to side, hold his balance and cut. He had power. He had strength. He had finesse. He had the speed and the passing ability. There were no flaws in his game. He scored two or three goals that night.

I had thought George Weah was the best player I would ever see in person. And then I saw Ronaldo — he's one of the top five players of all time. He did stuff that inspired Ronaldinho, Messi, Neymar, and everyone who came after him. It made it easier to stomach my situation. Ronaldo is why I couldn't play for Barcelona? Okay, I could handle that. If they hadn't signed him and were able to sign me, who knows what would've happened?

That experience helped shape me. I was so confident heading into the 1997 CONCACAF U-20 Championships in Mexico. I won the Golden Boot. I was getting noticed. Duke University and all of these colleges were coming after me. And then I saw that SAT book.

I was a big fan of education, but I wasn't a big fan of school. Growing up, I was in special education for a stretch. The only thing I liked about school was gym class, so the idea of trying to be a collegiate athlete wasn't very appealing. I had the book but never took my SATs. I was planning to, until I actually started reading it. When I looked at that book I saw years of my life passing by.

There were five of us living in a two-bedroom apartment. I didn't want to ever ask anyone for money again. I wanted to be in a position to make my own and take care of the people I cared about most. After not signing with A.C. Milan or FC Barcelona, I felt like I had let my dad down. He didn't think that way, but I did. So I told my dad, I wanted to quit high school and go after this dream. And he let me do it.

Bruce had assembled a great team to take to Malaysia in 1997. We were unlucky to draw Spain in the second round and lose. But I had made my mark. We were on the other side of the world, playing games in the middle of the night, but I was getting noticed. Before that tournament, I had started playing in the A-League with Toronto Lynx. I was on a game-by-game contract. Toronto was my world, but I knew it wasn't *the* world. Craig Forrest was doing well in the Premier League. Frank Yallop was in England too, at Ipswich Town, and Alex Bunbury was playing in Portugal. Canadian players had started to get opportunities overseas. I wanted mine.

I had had so many close calls; I needed to prove that I wasn't just a flash in the pan, a Canadian kid with flare. I wanted to make a name for myself and prove I could play in Europe, and I could play anywhere. Second division German club FSV Zwickau wanted both me and my Canadian teammate Jason Bent. It seemed perfect. I called him and said, "I know it's not A.C. Milan, it's not Barcelona. It's East Germany man, and that might be a tough place for guys like you and me. But if you're in, I'm in, bro."

J.B. was in. Book it. We were going to Germany, baby.

CHAPTER 5

MAKING IT

My old coach Barry Maclean knew some football agent who worked with German clubs. We had no representation. I never had an agent up to that point. The coach of Zwickau had watched us play with Canada at the 1997 U-20 World Cup in Malaysia and contacted this agent because of his North American connections.

"Sign with him, and he'll take care of you," Barry told Jason and me, presenting it as the perfect opportunity to kick-start our professional careers.

Everything happened fast. Jason and I were on a plane to Germany just a couple of days after Barry had reached out. We flew out together and joined the team at this training camp in the countryside. I was really happy to have someone to go with. I really didn't know what to expect at all. German soccer wasn't on TV very much.

We arrived at night and trained with the first team in the morning. Morning sessions are hard enough as it is, but jet-lagged training sessions are something else. Luckily, we fit right in, like we'd already been there for weeks. The coach really liked us. He was excited by all the little things we did. We ate a team meal and then Jason and I were taken back to Zwickau with a couple of officials. The rest of the players stayed at this countryside camp. When we got to the team offices, they presented both of us with a contract. After just one session, they liked what they saw and wanted to tie us down. I was hesitant. Things usually didn't happen that fast. The money was good, six figures, and the terms seemed reasonable. But we hadn't even seen the town yet. We didn't really know what we were getting into. I wanted to sleep on it and at least walk around in the day time. Jason agreed to sleep on it.

Holy shit, this town could fit in the palm of my hand. We got up at 9 a.m. and headed out on our own. Nothing was really open. I started getting goosebumps and getting nervous. J.B. was confident — he wanted the chance as much as I did. He was going to sign the deal. I said, "I came here with you, and I'm not going to leave here without you. If you're gonna sign, then I'm gonna sign too."

If it weren't for Jason, I wouldn't have signed. I wasn't really feeling it. In all my other experiences, you had time to settle in and feel like you got to know more than just the training pitch. We hadn't even seen the stadium during the day or talked to all of our teammates. As soon as we put pen to paper, they put us back in a car and took us to the Czech Republic to get our visas. Everything was very . . . efficient.

Germany had been unified for a few years. It was one Germany now. But we realized pretty quickly, there were still two.

The headline in the local newspaper read, "FSV Sign Two Dread-locked Jamaicans." Jason thought that was funny. I didn't. I was proudly Guyanese. But was this how they perceived us? "The dark ones." There was a Russian goalie and one or two other guys who were from the Eastern Bloc. But we were the only two minorities. The team was very East German.

When we first arrived, the players were cool with us. But everything changed during those first few days. Jason and I hadn't even featured in a real game yet, but it was clear the attitude had shifted within the change room. The players were disgruntled with us and mad at the coach for signing us. Maybe they were jealous that he thought so highly of us.

Maybe they didn't like that we were now a part of their team. I don't know, but they definitely made us feel like we were alone.

Our pre-season games were held in these smaller villages. These fans were relentless. I had heard a few racial insults in Toronto in my time, but it was never malicious. I had never heard anyone use the N-word as freely as some of those fans. It was crazy. And it was constant. We would go out to dinner with foreign players from visiting teams just to literally console each other.

"Yo, we just got here. Is it like this all the time?"

"Yes, brother! It is like this all the time."

Our own fans would chant monkey noises at Jason and me and throw bananas on the pitch. I was getting hit with coins and lighters almost every game. I felt bad. This was hardcore shit. Because you weren't one of them, they had to treat you differently.

We would go to West Germany all the time. The team had given us a sponsored car, a sporty Opel sedan. We went to every reggae show we could find. There was a big reggae festival in Frankfurt one year that must have drawn half a million people from all over. When we had downtime, we'd hit the Autobahn and fly up and down the country, looking for things to do. Racing cars in Leipzig became a monthly tradition. Ferraris. Aston Martins. You name it, we drove it. Other than that, we had to get out of East Germany as much as we could, just to keep our sanity.

The team was doing okay. But when we showed up, the players completely turned on the coach. He had no control of the change room. The guys wouldn't follow his directions and were noticeably tuning him out all the time. Even our opposition noticed it. The coach resigned after a couple of months. That was literally the worst thing that could've happened for Jason and me.

Everything went downhill after that. The club hired a hard-nosed East German guy who had worked with many of the players before. He literally didn't say a word to us in months, not even in German. It's one thing to train while knowing you could still play; it's another thing to know that you don't have a chance. Jason and I were getting called up to the Canadian national team, but we couldn't get minutes in 2. Bundesliga. It was problematic.

Despite having a coach the team liked, the results only got worse. So did morale. We were getting in scraps with teammates, and everything became so intense, you didn't know if you were going to get kicked in line at the cafeteria or decked in the shower. Even Jason and I got into a fight playing a six-versus-six game. It was so bad, we were fighting with each other. That night I called my dad for the first time in a while. It was expensive to call home back then. You saved those calling card minutes for when you really needed them.

"Dwayne! It's been a minute, son. How are things . . . "

"I can't wait to get out of here, Pops. There's no life here."

It was the first time I had said that out loud to someone other than Jason. He told me I couldn't leave until I at least had a heart-to-heart with my coach. He was right. I didn't want this to be another "What if?" moment in my life.

The next day, I showed up early to training so I could catch the coach alone in his office. It was the only way I knew I could force him to talk to me. Neither of us wanted to chat, so I was blunt.

"Look, I don't know what your intentions are, but since you came here, you haven't said a word to us. You don't name us to the team; we don't travel with the guys. Just be straight with me. What's our future here? If there's not one, we want to go."

He seemed to appreciate my honesty.

"Dwayne, I like your mentality and that you are brave enough to come talk to me. I like that you have that drive, and you are hungry and angry you are not playing. I like that you want a chance. I am going to put you on in the second half of the next game. It's a home game and it's really important for us. We need to win."

That wasn't the reaction I was expecting. The game was going to be on TV, and we really needed the points. Big moments — I live for them.

Like most games that season, the team was struggling. We were down 1–0 at halftime. I was ready to get my chance to change the game. It felt like the longest halftime of my life. The trainer came around to get the substitute bib and walked right past me. He grabbed the player next to me and told him he was going on to start the second half. Okay, not my turn. We walked out for the second half and I took my seat back on the bench. We were playing as bad as we were in the first half. I was just watching and waiting. Ten minutes went by, then 15, then 25. Finally, Coach called me.

"Here we go. Here's my time," I thought. He put me on the wing. I never played wing. My first few seconds on the field, we gained possession on the left side, and my own teammate 10 feet away fired the ball right at my nuts. Professionals don't make mistakes like that.

I knew what he was doing. I should've just let the ball go out. But I tried to control it and turned it over. Their player took off. I chased the man back up the field, stole the ball off him, and started running back on offense. But, being the stubborn man that I was, I had to return the favour to my teammate. He was standing about 15 feet away, so I blasted the ball back at him, right at his knees. The opposition picked it up and took off the other way. My whole team was yelling at me. I just stared at the guy.

The ball went out for a corner kick, and the substitution sign went up. It was my number. I'd been on the pitch for only 90 seconds, and Coach was burning one of our three substitutions to take *me* off!

I subbed out and walked straight to the change room. I took off my kit, got in my car, and left. I didn't even take a shower. Enough was enough. I had to get out of there.

Thankfully, Jason felt the same way, so the next morning we called a meeting with the coach and the club president. It was time to have an honest conversation about how to walk away from this situation that wasn't working for anybody, in a way that worked for everybody.

"It's clear that you want to leave and this is not working. But we can't let you go. We paid too much money for you."

That was our introduction to the ugly side of football.

"What? Who did you pay?"

We were free transfers. We weren't owned by any club. Apparently, good old Barry Maclean had written up a contract to negotiate our sale to Zwickau before we arrived. This is why the club was so quick with our player contracts. Barry had drawn up some formal sale saying that Jason and I were "high-profile Canadian internationals." Zwickau thought they were paying Canada Soccer to acquire us.

Now, we were really fucked.

We couldn't get ahold of Barry or the agent. To this day, I have no clue how much they walked away with.

The winter break was approaching. I told Jason I was buying a one-way ticket home and I wasn't coming back. He warned me not to do it, said it would ruin my career.

"What else am I gonna do, bro? Stay here and die?"

This was not the international football experience I envisioned. Germany was supposed to work out. It was supposed to be what all those experiences I had before weren't. If this was what it was like to play in Europe, I didn't want any part of it.

Jason had played NCAA soccer at the University of Maryland, so he had made a name for himself in the States already. He came back to North America, and within a month he signed with the Colorado Rapids. But nobody really knew me outside of that U-20 World Cup in Malaysia. I was in limbo. Maybe professional soccer wasn't for me.

I took a job at The Big Carrot, a health food store. I was at a real low point and at that same crossroads again. I couldn't live the life I wanted to live by working retail. I was getting sucked back into that street life. It didn't matter what I had gone through with my eye or what I had seen of the world. Here I was again, debating, "Do I want the street life hustle to be my life?"

There were a lot of people making real money on the streets. It seemed so easy for some. They had everything money could buy, but they couldn't enjoy living. Each day could have been the end of it all. A handful of my childhood friends were serving hard time in jail. I didn't want to go to jail, and I didn't want to be dead. I needed to make soccer work.

Word got around that I had left Germany. Nick De Santis from the Montreal Impact called me. They were A-League at the time, like

Toronto Lynx, but I didn't want to play in Canada. My Auntie was getting old, and her health was getting bad. If I stayed at home, I couldn't make the money I needed to help out and live the way I wanted to live. I was watching J.B. at Colorado. I wanted to play Major League Soccer (MLS). Then I got a call from the Richmond Kickers. I don't know how they got my number, but I knew they played in the second tier of the American soccer pyramid and were affiliated with D.C. United.

Virginia was hot. I showed up to the training ground and saw Jamaican internationals Onandi Lowe and Gregory Messam. These guys played on the Reggae Boyz team that went to the World Cup in 1998. Gary Glasgow, a Trinidad and Tobago international, was there too. This team had some real Caribbean flavour. I liked it from the start.

There was one spot in town we liked to go to a lot because they had a weekly reggae night. You can imagine when I moved out there, I didn't expect to find any place that reminded me of home. But for one night a week, it was like I was clubbing in Scarborough. Only this time, nobody had to steal a car to get us there.

One night we were there with some Virginia Commonwealth University (VCU) players. They were hanging out with some girls I had never seen before. There was one I couldn't take my eyes off of: Brandy. I was hanging out in a booth with my teammates and she eventually walked past me. "Oh, you've finally decided to come talk to me?" I teased.

"I'm just going to the bathroom."

This girl made me work. She told me she had a boyfriend and wouldn't give me her number. But she gave me her email address. A few months went by and I'd see her at those reggae nights. She was living in D.C. but had a part-time job in Richmond. Soon enough, she broke up with that guy and let me take her on a date. Richmond is a romantic little place. I took her down to the James River, and we talked for hours. I had never met anyone like her.

She couldn't have cared less that I was a pro soccer player. The weather was awful during the first game she came to. She hated it.

"People really do this? They come out and stand in this mess to watch *soccer*?"

There were no sports fans in her house. Her parents were Black nationalists. Her mother was a Rastafarian, who'd had dreadlocks for most of Brandy's childhood. She grew up in a home with vegetarians, so picking date spots was easy for me because I had been a vegan since I was 14. But we didn't have too many date nights. She had just graduated from VCU and went off to Senegal to study dance. I knew she didn't expect to see me again. But I couldn't keep her off my mind. I found out where she was and called her in Senegal. She was staying in this fishing village that literally had one phone.

"Brandy, you got a phone call!"

She thought it was her mom.

"No, it's a guy."

She couldn't believe it was me. I couldn't believe I actually found something to focus on other than soccer and my diet. She came back to the States a couple of months later and moved in with me in Richmond. Everything was really coming together for me. I was training harder and eating better than I had in my entire life.

I was in monk mode, something I learned from my teammate Roger Thomas. He was my roommate when I first moved to Richmond, and he showed me how to focus my time and energy on my game, while leaving a little bit of time to round out my life.

In my second year, Richmond drew Jason Bent's Colorado Rapids in the second round of the U.S. Open Cup. What are the chances of that? There were 32 teams in the competition at this point. Of all the matchups that could've been, it was me versus Jason. Like I say, everything happens for a reason.

I mashed up the Rapids. Our team played great, and I got plenty of service. I felt like I could really play *my* game that night, and that got me noticed. I knew Colorado was surprised and started asking Jason about me. And when one person starts talking about your skills, five people start talking, and it just grows from there.

Knocking off an MLS side was a big deal for a second division team like Richmond. The tournament was starting to get a lot of notoriety, and it was becoming a real showcase for players who were looking to make the step up to MLS. I had proven I could play against guys at that level. It was time for me to make a move. I was focused on using the rest of the season as my showcase.

Our next game back in Richmond was around July 4th weekend. There was a great vibe in town, and everyone on the team was feeling nice. I walked into the locker room and spotted a new guy sitting there: Mike Burke from D.C. United. They had sent him down to play with us. Our manager, Leigh Cowlishaw, introduced him to the team.

"Guys, this is Mike. He's going to be playing with us for the next little while. Make him feel welcome. He'll slide right into the system tonight and start up front next to DeRo."

I wish I could've seen the look on my face when Leigh said that. I stood up and said, "I'm not playing."

"What? What do you mean you're not playing?"

"I'm not playing if he's playing. This guy comes down from D.C. United and steps right into the starting eleven? All of us in here are busting our asses, and they're not calling us up. If he's playing, I'm not playing."

I don't think anybody knew how to react. Mike had a look on his face like a kid who has just caught his parents fighting and tries to blend in with the furniture. I definitely saw a few jaws drop. Someone mumbled, "DeRo . . . what are you doing, bro?" Leigh begged me to go into his office. I waited a second, looked at everybody in the room, and then followed Leigh around the corner.

"Dwayne, come on. Listen, we're affiliated with D.C. They sent me this guy because he's coming off an injury and he needs playing time."

Leigh was a 30-year-old head coach. They had just given him the head coaching job that season after playing for six years with the team. He was a part of Richmond's inaugural season in 1993, so the club succeeding meant the world to him.

"Boss, we've been busting our asses down here. We're through to the third round of the U.S. Open Cup. Everything is going good in the room right now. They can't just drop some guy in here like we don't have our own thing going on. They never give us an opportunity. How come we gotta open our doors to them?"

I knew he was in a tough spot. He was a young guy trying to prove to himself, his team, and the brass that he could handle everything that came with managing. And he was good at it. He was a guy everybody liked playing for.

"Dwayne, I respect you. Really, I respect what you're trying to do. It takes some balls. But we're a pro club trying to build an affiliation with the bigger club. We need to build this relationship, and right now this is what they've asked us to do. Who knows, at the end of the year maybe you can go up to D.C.?"

"At the end of the year, I fucking better be going up to D.C. Or I'm not coming back to Richmond," I told him. He nodded. At this point, he was probably expecting that answer.

"Go out and play your game tonight. They're watching. And hey, if it means anything, I'm going to put in a good word for you. You really would be a great addition to their team."

I don't remember how that game finished. Mike fit in with the team pretty quickly and went on to play 12 seasons with the Kickers. We lost to my old Toronto Lynx in the Eastern Conference semifinal that year. It's always a pain to lose to your old team, but I was happy for the guys I knew in that room.

For the first time in five MLS seasons, D.C. United missed the play-offs. They had won three of the first four MLS Cups, and missing the playoffs was unthinkable at the start of the year. At the end of the 2000 season, D.C. United invited me and a few other trialists to El Salvador. Greg Simmons and Adrian Serioux, who was playing with Toronto Lynx at the time, got the call too. I was happy to head down there with another Canadian and a guy I knew really well.

Finally, I was playing with MLS guys. And two of the best to have ever played in the league: Jaime Moreno and Marco Etcheverry. These guys were legends. The league had only been around for five years, and they had led D.C. to three championships. They were the kings of MLS. I was out there training as hard as they were, and I don't think they expected me to be able to keep up. Those sessions were intense. It was a great professional set-up, even away on a building trip. I noticed they were starting to gravitate towards me. I did really well down there. I felt free, played my game, and didn't really think about what other people thought of me. I just knew if I played my game, good things would come.

Thomas Rongen, the head coach of D.C. United at the time, is one of the most colourful guys I've ever met. He has a way with words like nobody else, but he'll tell you it's because he speaks four languages and he's always mixing them up. This man lives and breathes soccer, and like me, cares deeply about its growth on this side of the world. I could tell he really liked me as a player. He was matching me up against his best defenders in drills and paired me with Jaime in mini games. Thomas showed a lot of faith in me on that trip and made me feel comfortable in their pro environment.

"Dwayne, we really like you, man. You've got a great style out there and we think you could really help us. We want to sign you."

This guy played with Johan Cruyff, one of the best and most impactful players our game has ever seen. When Thomas likes a player, it means something. He also knew how to pick a coaching staff. Canadian Frank Yallop had played for Thomas in Tampa Bay and joined him in D.C. as an assistant coach. Thomas knew it was just a matter of time before Frank was a manager himself. Towards the end of the trip, Frank pulled me aside after a meal.

"You've really done well on this trip. I know Thomas really likes you. But, hey, unless they show you a contract today and it's money you can retire on, stall on it. I may not be around here much longer. And where I'm going, I've got a place for you."

That was all I needed to hear. I didn't need to know where. I didn't need to know when. I trusted Frank and I knew he trusted me. We had been roommates on several national team trips in the past. If a team was going to make Frank their manager, I had to play for that team.

Two days before the MLS SuperDraft, the San Jose Earthquakes named Frank their fourth coach, after just five seasons in Major League Soccer. A founding team in 1996, San Jose had struggled to compete. Frank played three seasons with the Tampa Bay Mutiny, then coached with one of the best organizations in the league at D.C. United. He was fully deserving to finally take charge of his own club. I couldn't have been more excited for our San Jose journey to start.

I went down for the MLS Draft Combine, even though I wasn't draft eligible. San Jose had just hired Frank, so it was a busy time. Everything was moving pretty quickly for him. It was crazy to see just how much goes into assembling a team when you first take over. Frank had just hired Dominic Kinnear to be his assistant coach. Like Thomas Rongen, I think Frank knew Dominic would be a great head coach one day. I met Dominic for the first time on that trip, and I don't think either one of us could have imagined how much success we'd have together.

CHAPTER 6

TOP OF THE WORLD

I used to be a pyro kid. I would set anything on fire: wood, garbage, those stupid gnomes people keep in their gardens. If it could catch, I'd light it up. I had a friend who was into it too, and we used to battle to see who could light the biggest fire. One time, we lit a fire on the Scarborough Rapid Transit train tracks. The Toronto transit system has enough delays as it is, they don't need two stupid kids lighting their system on fire.

When I did those things, there was always a voice in the back of my mind asking, "What are you doing?" That was my conscience that my Aunt had instilled in me. I never lost that pyro urge. I just changed my outlet.

On the soccer field, I went out to seek and destroy from day one. Scarborough kids always had so much to prove. My upbringing taught me nothing comes easy. And when you grow up with little, when you finally get something, you want more. I arrived in San Jose at the perfect time.

Frank had taken over a team in 2001 that couldn't win. They had finished last place the year before and hadn't made the playoffs since the first year of MLS in 1996, when it was a 10-team league. The club started as the San Jose Clash but re-branded in 2000, taking the old

Earthquakes name from the famous North American Soccer League (NASL) club of the '70s and '80s. We shook up the league in 2001.

When you walk into a new situation, you need hungry guys, and you need winners. San Jose needed a total overhaul from top to bottom, and Frank knew exactly what he was doing. Defender Jeff Agoos was the perfect vet to bring in. He won three MLS Cups in D.C. and was still playing at the top of his game. He knew what it took to win in that league, and he had already been capped like a hundred times for the U.S. Men's National Team. Ramiro Corrales was another defender who came in and sparked the team. He had a great MLS career and retired in 2013 as the last player to have played in the league's first season. Frank traded for midfielder Manny Lagos at the draft, and 2001 was probably the best season of his career. I wasn't the only young guy up front. Frank brought in 19-year-old Landon Donovan too.

Landon was going to be the golden boy of American soccer. Like me, his first pro experience was in Germany. And like me, it didn't work out the way he had hoped. But Frank gave him a great opportunity to come back home to California and develop his game.

We had a luxury of options up front. Ronald Cerritos was in San Jose during the bad days. He was the team's top scorer for a few seasons, including 2001. He busted his ass in training just as hard as we did. He wasn't going to lose his place to a couple of young bucks. Frank did a really good job of managing all of us. He knew I hadn't followed him to San Jose to sit on the bench. And Landon hadn't left Bayer Leverkusen in Germany to watch from the sidelines. But Frank wasn't going to give Landon game time just because he was expected to. And he wasn't going to give me minutes just because I was Canadian and I was his guy. We had to earn that game time. That made those training sessions really intense. Landon and I had to work for every second out there. And that really pushed us to be better.

The first game of the season set the tone for the team. A California Clásico versus the LA Galaxy, San Jose's biggest rival. If you ask me, that's when the rivalry was born. Frank named me in his starting eleven, alongside Ronald. It was special to walk out on that MLS field for the first time, at the 100,000-seat Rose Bowl. There were less than twenty thousand fans there. But that didn't matter; this was the big time. This was the goal I was focused on, and now I had to deliver.

We couldn't have started better. Our defender Troy Dayak scored in the first 10 minutes. "Cowboy" didn't score many goals and he had dealt with some brutal injuries, so everybody was happy to see him score one. Ronald scored 15 minutes later. And then I had my chance. Twenty-seven minutes into my Major League Soccer career, and I was on the scoresheet. I was flying. We were three goals up in less than 30 minutes. But all that mattered was that we left the Rose Bowl with three points. LA got stronger as the game went on and bagged two late goals, but we held on and started the season with a statement win. San Jose wasn't no last place team anymore, not with Frank and me around.

I didn't know what to expect for our first game at home. Spartan Stadium was way more intimate than the Rose Bowl. It felt like a gladiator forum. There was a wall separating the stands from the field, so the fans looked down on to the pitch. A football field on the campus of San Jose State University, it was the Earthquakes' home from 1996 to 2005. But it was good to us, and we drew some great crowds. We lost that first game at home to Dallas, and my scoring streak stopped at one game. But I'd score my share of goals there.

In the U.S. soccer world, Landon had a lot of eyes on him, and that put pressure on Frank when picking the team. After starting the season well, I became the super-sub. My role was to come off the bench and cause havoc for the other team. I would terrify tired defenders. There weren't too many attackers at that time who would take on a player one-on-one or dribble down the field 25 yards to create their own chance. My whole focus every time I subbed in was to score or assist a goal. It didn't matter if I was on the pitch for only 10 minutes, or five minutes, or one minute. I had that goal in mind and I didn't let anything get in the way.

But it was frustrating just being the guy who might get a few minutes this game, maybe not the next. I wasn't satisfied with that role. The All-Star Game was in San Jose that year. Five Quakes were named to the West All-Stars, and I wasn't one of them. Landon scored a hat trick in the first 20 minutes and scored another goal late in the game. It ended in a 6–6 tie if you can believe it. Landon was Man of the Match, and deservedly so. But I knew that meant it was going to be even harder for me to get minutes. There were a lot of people in my ear saying, "DeRo, you should be starting man! They don't value you. You got to get out of there."

I'd be lying if I said I didn't hear them. But I blocked those people out. I let that inspire me instead of discourage me. Frank and Dom were transparent with me, and they always motivated me to keep working. That was crucial for me. Any time they could sense I was down, one of them would pull me aside and say, "Just keep doing what you're doing. The team sees how hard you're working, and it's making everyone work harder. That's what we need right now. You're a huge part of this team. Minutes aren't the only measurement for that. More minutes will come."

The standard in San Jose was so high. It was the most professional environment I had experienced up to that point in my life. I didn't want to take it for granted. Our group was very competitive — not only were we competing for minutes, we were competing against each other. Free kick challenges, cross bar contests, keep-ups. The loser had to buy the rest of the guys lunch or a smoothie. I hardly ever lost. I couldn't stand losing, and I wasn't about to buy Landon, Ronald, or anybody lunch. I had picked out my prize before we even decided which challenge we were going to do. Açaí, protein, and multivitamin, with whatever non-dairy milk they had.

———

San Jose is a beautiful place to live. The views are breathtaking. I used to ride my bike to training every day. It would take me 25 minutes each way — although the ride home usually took longer. Players would drive past me on their way in and ask, "What's the matter, bro? You don't wanna pay for gas?"

I wanted the extra training. I was in the best shape of my life and needed to stay that way. Eventually we changed training facilities, and I had to ditch the bike for the 30-minute drive. But I made up for it by running through the hills with my baby strapped to my chest in a baby carrier.

I related more to the veteran guys. I wasn't a real rookie: I wasn't drafted out of college the year before, and I had already been on my own and playing pro for a few years. I was a dad already and had another kid on the way. But differences aside, the team had a bond that I truly appreciated. We would go out as a team, and the wives and girlfriends would get together all the time. There were a couple of club BBQs every year, and they really were for everybody: the grounds crew was there, the stadium staff brought their families out, the front office got to kick back and hang with the players. It always turned into a classic Scarborough cookout, just without the West Indian food. We were a family, and it reminded me of my Malvern Magic days. Not every group is like that.

Frank is such a chill manager. He knows how to manage individual players. Everyone has an ego, and everyone has their own strengths and weaknesses. Frank is able to get the most out of his players by making them believe they're better players than they actually are. And when they believe it, they're able to embody it. That's why he's so well respected in the game.

All the players took it so personally when we lost because we felt like we had let Frank and Dom down. We didn't lose very often. But after the All-Star break we dropped two in a row, and for the first time, the mood in the room was really down. All of a sudden, the little things that were going right before weren't.

The next training session after a loss is always intense. We walked into the locker room the next morning, and the training kits weren't laid out. The room looked like it hadn't been touched. I asked the equipment manager what was going on.

"Frank said not to put the gear out today. I don't know why."

Damn. That was a first. We were expecting the worst. Some of the guys thought Frank was going to make us wear garbage bags and run up and down Spartan Stadium's concrete steps for two hours. I was afraid they might be right. Every player was in the room when Frank walked in dragging a big bag. We were dead silent. He dropped it in the middle of the room for everyone to see. It was filled with baseball gloves and baseballs. One for everybody. We were so confused.

"Each one of you, grab a glove and go out there and throw the ball around. We don't need to run drills today."

Baseball? Ain't nobody wants to play baseball at a time like this. We all wanted to get out there, kick some ass, and get ready for Saturday.

Frank walked out of the room, and it took a minute before the first guy reached in and grabbed a glove. We went down to the field and started throwing balls around. At first it felt stupid, like a waste of everybody's time. But then there were smiles all around. Next, everybody was laughing. All of a sudden, we were joking around and having a good time. It had been a couple of weeks since we had felt like that around each other. Instead of making us run and hammering us, Frank did the complete opposite. He knew that overthinking things could do more harm than good. We didn't think much of it in the moment, but we all left that training session feeling good. I think I rode my bike home in 26 minutes that day. I walked in the door, grabbed Brandy, and gave her a big hug and a kiss.

"What the hell did you get up to today? You were one miserable-ass man when you left this morning."

"We played baseball today. Everything's good."

I don't think she believed me.

When you lose, it's impossible not to bring that home with you. It's one of the things our families have to put up with as "part of the job."

That year, Brandy was introduced to life as a pro athlete's wife. When I knew I was leaving Richmond to follow Frank, she packed up her life in a duffle bag and got on a plane. She had just finished school, left her job, sold her car, and got rid of everything in Richmond. My wife was always up for an adventure. That's how she was able to pull off so many moves. But that first move was the most intense. She was pregnant.

Our son Osaze was born on July 19, 2001. I became a different man that day. It's true when people say your priorities change when you become a father, and with each new child you have. I remember putting him to sleep on my chest that first night, telling him that he was going to do great things and would motivate me to do great things. He was my first son. That really sparked something in me. And I wasn't the only player to have a child that year; there were a few in the group. It became a good luck motto for the team. "Babies bring championships."

Halfway through the season, we knew we had a team good enough to make a run at the MLS Cup. We were a strong group from front to back, and everybody in that room had something to prove. The new guys wanted to show they belonged, and the guys who were on those losing San Jose teams wanted to prove they were better. We had lost only twice at home in the regular season. We rolled through Columbus in the first round. In the next round, a golden goal from "Cowboy" against Miami booked our ticket to the title game.

We were off to the 2001 MLS Cup Final. All the shit I had been through in Germany. All the work I had put in up to that point. All the things my wife and I had to deal with as new parents. This was the fruit of that labour. Not once did I ever think we weren't going to win the final in Columbus, Ohio. It wasn't an ordinary championship game though.

America was in a very different place. The final was played less than six weeks after 9/11. The season was shortened by a few games because all professional sports leagues shut down after the attacks. Travelling had become such a pain. I was always getting pulled to the side because border patrol and security could never figure out what nationality I was. Canadian didn't count. I didn't fit a typical profile, which meant I had to be profiled.

There was a lot of fear in America at that time. There was a lot of anger. When we got to Columbus, someone from the league's security team told all the minority guys to stay in the hotel unless we were travelling with the entire team to and from the stadium. I thought he was joking. We were in Columbus in the 2000s, not in the 1800s. We didn't know that there was going to be a Ku Klux Klan rally in the city that week. It passed right in front of our hotel. There were more people there than I expected — we heard them for hours. Coming from Canada, that was the last thing I thought I would ever see with my own eyes. It was messing with my emotions. What world had I just brought my son into?

There was a huge military presence everywhere that weekend. We showed up to the stadium for training, and the military dogs walked through the team bus and checked all the bags. We stepped off, and there was a long line of soldiers strapped with M16s, standing guard. Everybody was on high alert. There was a fear that something might happen during the game. It was kind of scary.

I was supposed to be preparing for the biggest game of my life, and there I was worrying about the state of the world.

The night before the game, I sat down in my room, thinking I had to do something. As athletes, we have so much power and so much say. All the ignorance and fear surrounding me was driving me crazy. I wanted people to know that going to war to kill more people wasn't the only option. In times like these, we needed to bring people together. And then it hit me: Bob Marley.

I wrote "One Love" on my undershirt. It was a little extra motivation to score, so that I could pull my jersey over my head and reveal it.

There's nothing quite like the week of a final. There are 10 times more media around. The fans have travelled halfway across the country to cheer you on. Your family flies in from all over because they want to be there for your big moment. The game is on national TV. The Commissioner is around, and everything feels official. There's so much going on, it can be overwhelming.

I never really felt pressure, I just felt the anticipation. I couldn't sleep at night, and I was antsy during the day. I would walk up and down the stairwells in the middle of the night. But I'd look at a guy like Jeff Agoos, who played in World Cups and MLS Finals, and he was calm. I realized I needed to be more like that. Frank talked to me after dinner the night before the game.

"DeRo, I know how much you want to play tomorrow. I'm going to try to get you into the game at some point. Just be ready."

The LA Galaxy were the perfect test for us. We were a collection of guys who had willed our way to the final. We weren't supposed to be there: San Jose was the worst team in the league the year before and had been completely revamped under a new coach. We made the biggest turnaround in MLS history at the time. And we had beat LA twice in the regular season. All the pressure was on them.

Walking onto that field for warm-ups was something else. You could literally smell the importance of that game. Columbus Crew Stadium was packed, and there was a big group of fans who had come from San Jose. Their team had never made the playoffs before — they weren't about to miss the final. Some of them drove twenty-five hundred miles to be there. LA had a big fan base, so there was a lot of that ugly yellow and green in the stands too.

The importance of the game swept over me again when the referee blew his whistle at kickoff. We were 90 minutes away, or a little more, from potentially being champions. We started well. The boys set the tone and kept possession for the first 20 minutes. And then LA's Greg Vanney picked out Luis Hernández with a perfect 40-yard pass. "El Matador" put LA in front with a great finish. He was a clinical goal scorer for Mexico, and now he was showing American soccer just how good he was. We weren't shook. We stuck to our game plan. Just before halftime, Richard Mulrooney blasted the ball across the box, and it bounced right in front of Landon. He hit it on the volley with his right foot and put it in the top corner. It was a superstar's goal. And we were tied.

I was waiting for my moment to come in the second half. Whenever I warmed up, I would look down the bench and just stare at Frank until we made eye contact. I wasn't really warming up. I was fake stretching. Finally, he looked at me.

"DeRo! You ready?"

Of course I was ready. I had been waiting for that moment my whole life. My Milan and Barcelona chances had come and gone. This was the universe giving me the chance to make up for all of that. The substitution sign went up in the 85th minute. No. 20, Cerritos, off. No. 14, De Rosario, on. Frank put his hand on my shoulder and said, "This is your moment. You wanted it. You got it."

I felt like Donovan Bailey sprinting onto that field. I took my position, closed my eyes for a second, and said to myself, "Don't fuck this up." I felt more of a responsibility because I was Canadian and because my coach was Canadian: I was out there on that field representing all Canadians. I couldn't be mediocre.

Neither team scored another goal in the second half. We went to overtime tied 1–1. Back then, OT was golden goal, like in hockey — you score, you win.

I never liked playing in front of the defender or having them on my back. So I always drifted off to the left side. I saw Ronnie Ekelund looking at me as I peeled. He gave me the perfect pass. I collected the ball and saw LA's Danny Califf in front of me. He backed up as I dribbled towards him. I wanted him to dive in so I could touch it to my right foot and hit it with power. He was a good defender, so he wasn't going to bite. He just kept backing up. I took him in with my shoulder, and he moved just enough so I could see the space to shoot. Bang.

When you hit a ball in a match like that and you know it's going in, your stomach just drops. LA goalkeeper Kevin Hartman stretched out as far as he could and just got his fingers on it. But I had put too much will on that ball. It hit the inside of the post and bounced into the back of the net. We were MLS Cup champions. I had scored the golden goal.

The stadium exploded. Every white shirt on that field rushed towards me. As soon as I saw the ball bulge the net, I knew this was my chance. I pulled my jersey over my head to show off my "One Love" message. I did my shake 'n bake shuffle celebration and tried to keep my teammates off me long enough for the cameras to see my shirt. The boys piled on me. I broke away to find Frank. I needed to give him the biggest hug.

"That was for you!" I said as we wrapped our arms around each other at midfield.

Frank had given me my shot. He had brought me to San Jose and put me in the position to change that game. And we did it.

The TV cameras swarmed us. Everybody wanted their moment with us. We just wanted a moment with each other.

I didn't like talking to reporters and having a camera in my face on the field. I didn't like it when they made it all about me. But I had the microphone and I had something to say. I didn't want to talk about the goal or the championship; I wanted to talk about my shirt and the people who were dying because our leaders think wars are solutions. I wanted to show how sport unifies people. Look at all the different races on my team, celebrating with each other after achieving one common goal. But they didn't want to hear any of that. I got drowned out in all the celebration.

That wasn't the way I wanted to leave the stadium. I didn't really get to celebrate that championship the way I wanted to. We walked back to the team bus with a military escort and went to the hotel to celebrate with a team meal. No families, no outside friends. Just the team.

I went up to my room to shower and change. I put my championship medal on one side of the bathroom sink and my MLS Cup MVP trophy on the other side. I looked at myself in the mirror and just started crying. All my experiences had culminated to this moment. I was feeling so many emotions and had to let it out: tears of happiness, tears of sadness. We had just pulled off what so many people thought was impossible. The Earthquakes had gone from worst to first. With a Canadian coach and a Canadian golden goal scorer. It was incredible.

It's hard to follow that up. The next season we played in the CONCACAF Champions League for the first time. I had played in Mexico with the national team, but it was my first taste of club football down there. It was intense. We crashed out in the quarter-finals to Pachuca. At least we can say we had lost to the champions. It's not really a consolation, but it does sound better.

Fighting on two fronts was a challenge. We had a deep team and we had improved as a group. Everyone was a year older and more experienced. But the 2002 World Cup happened in the middle of the season. Jeff and Landon were away with the U.S. National Team, and they were stars in South Korea. A few guys on the team would get together to watch the games in the middle of the night. Beating Portugal was such a big moment for U.S. Soccer, and knocking out Mexico was an even bigger step. Landon introduced himself to the world with that World Cup. I wanted to be over there with Canada and have that moment. After winning the Gold Cup in 2000, everyone thought Canada would qualify for South Korea and Japan. I was happy for Jeff and Landon, and the better the U.S. National Team did, the better it was for MLS. But I hated that I was at home watching those games on TV.

The Quakes made the MLS Cup Playoffs again, and we played Columbus in the conference semifinals. I think we all had the same feeling: "We won here before. We'll just do it again." But we didn't. The Crew beat us 2–1 at home and 2–1 away. A few weeks later, LA Galaxy beat the New England Revolution, in New England's stadium, to win their first MLS Cup. We had a chip. Now they had a chip. That made our rivalry even better.

Whenever I'm in California, someone stops me to talk about 2003. We brought in a few new guys and were the best team in the West. LA was lucky to make the playoffs — they wouldn't have if they were in the East — and that a hamstring injury kept me out of the lineup. It was a dream first-round matchup for us. LA wasn't playing like a championship team, and we were ready to take back our throne.

We hated LA. We always played the Galaxy with a chip on our shoulder because we felt like they always got the love and got more games on TV. They were the big market team the league wanted to do well. The fans disliked each other, and the teams embraced that. There was nothing like those California Clásicos. It was the first derby experience that mattered, in my eyes. Everybody wanted to see San Jose versus LA Galaxy.

That first leg in Carson, they remembered they were the defending champions. They beat us 2–0. Going home, we were confident we could turn it around in the second leg. Spartan Stadium was ready for a fight that night. The fans were all over LA's players. The vibe during warm-ups was one of the best I'd seen. Carlos Ruiz scored seven minutes in. A few minutes later, Peter Vagenas doubled the Galaxy's lead. Fuck. The team that scores more goals away from home advances, so now we needed four goals, just to tie them on aggregate!

Jeff Agoos was pissed. He knew we were better than that and he was yelling at all of us to make sure we knew that too. He stepped up and scored a great free kick to get us on the scoreboard: 4–1. He didn't celebrate, he just had that "if you want something done, you gotta do it yourself" look on his face. Then Landon got one: 4–2. A wave came over the whole team: let's just give it everything we have. We couldn't quit on the fans and we couldn't quit on ourselves after the year we had. Let's just go for it. We came out in the second half, and young Jamil Walker headed home a free kick to narrow the lead, 4–3. Down 4–0, they thought we were dead and buried. Not a chance. I knew right then, we were going to win that game.

It got to stoppage time, and you could feel the anticipation in the building. Everyone was on the edge of their seat. The Galaxy were on their heels, wishing the referee would just blow his whistle. And then Thor Roner scored off his blond head. We had clawed our way back from a four-goal deficit to take the Galaxy to overtime. You could see on LA's faces, they were already beat. Faria scored the golden goal for us to finish them off. I guess it had to end that way.

It was the greatest comeback in MLS playoff history. Landon called it the greatest game he ever played in. That's saying something. There was no stopping us after that.

Two weeks later, we were back in LA's brand new stadium for the MLS Cup Final. It was a big deal when they built that place because it was built just for soccer. We really wanted to be the first team to win a championship on that field, but everyone had counted us out. Chicago Fire won the Supporters' Shield, the team with the best regular-season record, and had their own American World Cup stars. Chicago's Carlos Bocanegra and DeMarcus Beasley had signed to play in Europe at the end of the season, and everybody was talking about them, which was fine with us. We loved being the underdogs. Our fans filled the stands with "We Believe" signs. Every player in our locker room believed we were going to win that game, and Landon made sure he was the American player everybody was talking about at the end, scoring a goal in the first half. We had a 3–2 lead with 30 minutes to go when Frank looked down the sideline at me, fake stretching, waiting for my moment.

"DeRo! You ready?"

Of course I was ready. Before the game, I had written "One Love" on my undershirt again. It was my good luck charm. Chicago was getting confident and the crowd was behind them. I was ready to put an end to that. I ran the ball down the right side towards the corner and could see Landon running towards the net. I whipped in the perfect pass for him at the top of the six-yard box. All he had to do was tap it in: 4–2.

Landon came running towards me with the biggest smile on his face. He jumped right into my arms. We knew we had won the championship again. This time I celebrated like I wanted to. Well, maybe we could have celebrated in that locker room a little bit longer. We wanted the Galaxy to know we had won in their home.

Everything changed after that.

Frank took the Canadian Men's National Team job. He had won two MLS Cups with teams that nobody thought would win. Now he wanted to lead Canada to qualify for the World Cup in Germany, which few people outside the team thought he could do. Landon went back to Germany to finish out his contract at Bayer Leverkusen. I don't know why things didn't work out there for him, but when he wanted to come back to the States, he couldn't come back to San Jose.

The Galaxy wanted him to be their star piece. He was the face of American soccer, and he was from Southern California, so he wasn't leaving Europe for any place but where his family was.

When you go to your team's rival, you go from hero to zero real quick. Earthquakes fans were really harsh to Landon for signing with LA. Almost too harsh. He had accomplished so much in San Jose and had made his name as an Earthquake. I feel like those fans respected that, but they couldn't let him know that. They cursed him and heckled him for 90 minutes every time we played them. Landon playing for the Galaxy really intensified the rivalry. It made for a great environment to play in.

When Landon left, it was my time to step up. That's when I really started to recognize my place in the league. I started to feel like a star. People wanted more DeRo: I was doing commercials and being asked to do more interviews. I embraced it. I wasn't a young kid or a rookie anymore. I wanted to be the face of the team. "There was a kid from Scarborough, and DeRo was his name-oh . . . ." as the song goes.

Dominic Kinnear took over as head coach. It was perfect. He had learned from Frank during our run to two championships. He knew all the players, and he knew how to win. I went to him the first week of pre-season and told him I wanted to play as an attacking midfielder instead of a striker. I was already starting to drop in the hole a little bit to collect the ball. I was kind of worried he might not like my idea. I was wrong.

"Okay, let's give it a try."

From that point on, I played attacking mid behind Brian Ching and Ronald Cerritos. These guys were pros at holding the ball up. They used their bodies so well. I would time my pass and run right by them so they could play it back to me. I really started to enjoy playing that role because I was getting the ball a lot. When you play up top, you don't get as much of it. Now I was building the attack and was part of it. Brian and I developed a really good partnership. I would play to his strengths and he would play to mine. I'd take the midfielder to the left, then blast by him on the right. Then Brian would lay the ball back, first touch, right to me. Our opposition didn't know how to handle us.

Ricardo Clark stayed back and cleaned everything up. He was our workhorse. Rico is one of the best defensive midfielders I ever played with. His anticipation was his greatest value: he always knew how and where to position himself to win those balls. He wasn't flashy; he just knew his role and was very patient and calculated. He was like Michael Essien at the beginning. And most importantly, Rico gave me the ball a lot. I knew I could run up the field and he would hold it down. He was very underrated, but not in my books. I'd put Rico on any one of my teams. Bob Bradley took him to the 2010 World Cup in South Africa, but in my eyes he never got the respect he deserved from the U.S. National Team. And a lot of that probably had to do with his demeanour. Rico is cool like a deep freezer. If a coach yelled at him, he would respond with the most monotone, unfazed reaction every time: "My bad." He was the quietest guy, which made him a great roommate. He did lose his mind once though.

We were playing Dallas and our ex-teammate Carlos Ruiz was doing everything he could to get under Rico's skin. Carlos was smart and was really good at that. He was tripping himself up, kicking out, throwing elbows when the ref wasn't looking. Eventually Rico had enough. Carlos climbed over him on a corner kick and kneed him in the back as Carlos fell to the ground. He was lying face down on the grass, and Rico ran up and kicked Carlos right in the ribs. It turned into a giant street fight. I felt like I was with Boys in Blue again. You don't see that shit in soccer. I look back at that now and laugh; whatever Carlos did to get Rico to that point had to be some bad shit.

After we won the MLS Cup in 2003, there was all this talk that the owners would move the team. How could you move the team the year after we won the championship? They didn't. But over the next few years, the rumours remained. There was a big proposal for a new stadium that would solidify our roots in the Bay Area, but nothing ever came of that. We felt that at any moment we'd be told, "Tie things up in San Jose, guys. We're moving." I started to get really sick of it. The constant uncertainty made the team uneasy and affected our families as well.

Brandy and I took the kids to Jamaica at the end of the 2005 season. After losing to Landon's Galaxy in the playoffs and then watching them win the MLS Cup, we needed to get away. We spent two perfect days on the beach, and then I got an email from the team president. The Earthquakes were moving to Houston.

I was relieved. Not because I wanted to leave San Jose, but because it meant we could finally have stability again. Some guys on the team didn't like the idea of moving. Houston wasn't as appealing as the Bay Area to them. But for me, I was just thinking about soccer. I knew we were already a strong team, and a move like that would only bring us closer together. It was like we all got traded. And we all felt like shit about it.

The San Jose fans were great to us from the beginning. We had a thank you gala with season ticket holders just before Christmas. I remember seeing how sad they were. Their team was being stolen from them, and they took the move really hard. In any organization, the fans make the team. They make the players. They make us who we are. Some San Jose fans would fly down to Houston in those first couple seasons to support us. We really felt a connection with those fans, and we were grateful. But, we had to recreate ourselves as players, and as individuals, in a brand new place. We had to build a fan base in football country. American football.

Being a soccer team in Texas meant we were up against a lot. Soccer always has a fight.

The club flew all the players and their wives down to see what Houston was like. It was hot in December. I thought, "I can handle this." I scoped out all the vegetarian spots, the Jamaican spots. It didn't take me very long. The transition was intense: schools and houses had to change over Christmas, which is not an easy time to do anything. But it brought the guys together, and it really united us as a team. We became a very tight unit after that. Most of us bought homes in the same community, so we would carpool a lot and see each other walking with the kids and the dogs. That moving experience absolutely translated to our success on the field.

I wanted to make Houston a household name. The first game we stamped our name on the city. Robertson Stadium was packed. We were used to playing in a NCAA football stadium, so the only thing different for us was the heat. I poured a whole cup of water over my head before we took the team photo because I was already feeling it. If the crowd was too, it didn't sound like it. When Brian Ching first touched the ball off the kickoff, the crowd erupted like we had scored a goal. It took 13 minutes to make that happen. Wade Barrett passed me the ball and sprinted towards the top of the box. I hit him with the perfect pass, right along the carpet, just like Dad always taught us. He crossed it to the front of the net, and Brian was there to tip it home. Brian scored four goals in that first game. I assisted every one of them.

Although we had a lot of doubters, that first game proved that we were still the Earthquakes. But in orange shirts. We were disappointed with how 2005 ended, after losing to LA in the first round, and we carried that with us to Houston. That's why we had to come out of the gates flying, breaking records individually and as a team. We wanted to keep that momentum going in our new home.

That squad was such a competitive group, even more so than in San Jose. It was no nonsense. There was so much banter and competition during training, which would sometimes lead to a fight — no one liked to lose. The guys who saw that as a threat didn't last long. We pushed hard as hell at those early morning training sessions in 100-degree weather. That heat makes people crazy. My Scarborough came out in training once because I just didn't like that Eddie Robertson had slid in on me in training like I was the enemy. We didn't talk to each other for a day, but by the next session we had forgotten all about it — blamed it on the heat. Eddie was such a great defender, but he would always wild out. Whenever you saw a big tackle down the field, you knew it was him and you knew it was a red card. Then he'd cuss out the refs. It got him in trouble, but he was definitely one of those guys you wanted to have in the war with you.

That Houston heat got to all of our opponents. It affected them worse than us. We dealt with the heat in training, but it didn't affect us during games. So our approach from the start was to press the ball. Our televised games were always at 1 p.m. or 3 p.m. because the Astros played at night. That never made sense to me. The Astros had a roof on their ballpark. We were playing outside in "You shouldn't be outside" temperatures. The sun was just melting us into the grass, laughing at us like, "What the hell do you guys think you're doing out here? Are you stupid?" I never felt heat like that in my life.

I wore new shoes every game because I liked that tight, new feeling. By the end of the game, my shoes were begging to come off. They were smoking, they were so hot. Most games, I'd have to wear one pair in the first half and another pair in the second half. When you're sweating and running as hard as I was, you break them in quick. They were custom molded to fit my feet so it was easier. I loved my white boots, but I wore red boots when I played for Canada. I always wanted to have my own shoe. I would have made them affordable, like $30 to $35, so kids in communities like the one I grew up in could wear them. But those pitches fell on deaf ears with the big companies.

———

The support for us in Houston was unbelievable. The fan base really felt like we represented them and made us feel like we were Houstonians.

I'd take my wife out for dinner, and the bill would come as a "Thank you. Go Dynamo" written on a napkin. We would go to the mall and the fans would get so hyped, we'd have to be escorted by security. Once, when I was in the Puma store at Galleria shopping with my kids, one fan came in. Then a few more. Then the store was packed. The college kid working there looked at me and said, "Man, you gotta leave right now."

When I would take the kids to the park, fans would come up and ask me to autograph whatever they had on them: their kids' toys, their stroller, an American football.

Early in the season, a few of us went out one night after coming back from a road trip. We walked in the door of the club and they made us wait at the front.

"Just hold on a second guys and let us set up a table for y'all."

"We don't have a table. We're just gonna hang out for a little bit."

"You don't understand. Y'all's money ain't good here. We got you a booth; it's on the house. Here are a couple of bottles, and we'll get a couple of guys to stand guard near you so nobody bothers y'all."

That was some NBA-level stuff. That's how it was every time I went out in Houston. It was incredible, because a lot of people hated us before we even kicked a ball.

Choosing the right name is one of the most important things in life. All my children's names have a special meaning to my wife and me. The right name can be the difference between you being embraced right away or ignored. Same thing in sports. The Earthquakes' name belonged to San Jose. Houston's ownership group wanted a team name that meant something to the people of Houston. They wanted to put roots down in the city and make themselves part of the fabric of the community. So they used an online poll to choose the club's new name: Houston 1836. The name honoured the year the city was founded, and Major League Soccer wanted to get away from team nicknames that sounded really American.

Houston 1836 was cool. It sounded different. German clubs made that popular with 1860 Munich and Hanover 96. The problem was Houston 1836 pissed a lot of people off. 1836 was the year of the Texas revolution, when the state broke away from Mexico after an ugly and bloody war. The Latino community was offended, and they weren't going to support a club that was named after a dark time in their history. There was a huge protest when the team name was announced. When the players found out, a few of us spoke up.

"Look, this is offensive to people, and we can't be offending anybody right now. If they don't want us wearing "1836" on our shirts, then we don't want to be wearing it. This is the most important group, and we need them on our side in the beginning."

They had to pull the emergency brake on that real quick. Somebody dropped the ball big time, but you've got to give the owners credit for reacting to a mistake they'd made. Less than a month before the season kicked off, we became the Houston Dynamo.

"Dynamo" sounded powerful and was different. I loved the orange jerseys — something about them just popped, and you could spot one from anywhere. My braids hanging down the back of them looked badass. We were a badass team.

One of Dominic's greatest strengths as a coach is his ability to tap into guys who have a competitive spirit. He wanted guys who had that F-you mentality, who believed that no matter what, we were going to win. We always played to win. And that was unique.

I took more of a leadership role in Houston, mentoring the young guys. Dom and I would have conversations we never had before; I liked that he trusted me and consulted with me. I was very vocal in the locker room. I didn't care how the guys took it. I did it because I knew what needed to be done, and I knew we had to win. I wasn't sensitive to my teammates feelings. Fuck your feelings. If we needed to pick it up, I was gonna tell you. And I was just as hard on myself before I pointed any fingers.

Adrian Serioux arrived that first year in Houston. Dom asked me if I thought Adrian would be a good fit. There wasn't a doubt in my mind. Dom likes locker room guys who can motivate a room and change the mood. I knew Adrian was that guy. He was fun and he made things light. He fit into the team right away. He was the party captain and we had a lot of great nights thanks to him. We had played in Malvern together, and it was great to have someone I grew up with in Scarborough on the team. It was amazing that we both made it professionally and were on the same team, winning championships.

Everything came together that first year in Houston. We lost just three of our first 18 games. I started nearly every game that season and tied Brian Ching with a team-high 11 goals. After knocking off Chivas USA and Colorado in the playoffs, we booked our ticket to the 2006 MLS Cup Final, four hours up the road at FC Dallas' Pizza Hut Park. It was like a home game for us, and we painted the town orange. The fans couldn't have hoped for a better first season with us in town. It was the first final we played in where the crowd was really invested in one team. That definitely played to our advantage against New England.

The Revolution lost the year before to the LA Galaxy in that same stadium. They were out for revenge, especially Taylor Twellman. He won the league MVP award in 2005, by just a few votes ahead of me. He took the field with this possessed look in his eyes. I knew it well, because I had that same look in every final. He scored the first goal of the game, in the 112th minute. It wasn't golden goal anymore, so New England just had to outlast us for the final eight minutes. I'll never forget the look on his face as we kicked off again at the centre circle. He was convinced he had won his first championship. He was wrong. Brian Ching tied the game 42 seconds later. That was the winning goal for me because I knew they didn't have a chance at beating us in penalty kicks. They were level with us after 120 minutes, but mentally we were so much stronger.

Dom picked me to shoot third. We made our first two kicks, and so did they. New England's coach, Steve Nicol, chose goalkeeper Matt Reis to shoot second. Usually a goalie would shoot fifth or sixth, if at all. He kicked a perfect ball into the top right corner, past Pat Onstad. But now he had to settle back in and face me. I took all the time in the world walking up to the penalty spot. I couldn't hear a thing; I had blocked out the stadium noise completely. My head was silent. All I was thinking about was blasting that ball into the bottom left-hand corner. I spun the ball a few times on the spot before I stepped away from it. I wanted to make Matt wait so long that all of his confidence from scoring had disappeared. I took the slowest four steps backwards of my life and visualized the net bulging behind the keeper. The referee blew his whistle to shoot, and I let out a big exhale. Matt had guessed right, but I hit the ball so cleanly and put it so low, he couldn't get there. I had done my job.

I jogged back to the team to watch the rest. There wasn't any nervousness amongst us, just anticipation. It came down to New England's fifth shooter. Jay Heaps had to score to extend the shootout. I stood in between Stu Holden and Brian Ching as we watched with anticipation. When Jay ran up and kicked the ball, I think all of us said, "Nope." He hit a slow shot low, hoping to catch Pat guessing the wrong way. It was probably the easiest but most important save Pat made in his career. We were MLS champions again. After everything we had been through, after everything we had put our families through, we had been rewarded.

I couldn't wait to celebrate with my family. My son Adisa had just turned two. He chose that day to give my wife the hardest day of her life. At that age, a lot of days might feel like that, but this day, he was possessed. He was shitting up a storm. I don't think Brandy sat in her seat for 10 straight minutes during that entire final. He had her up and down, changing his diaper and his clothes constantly. By the end of the game, she was out. No diapers left. No clean clothes. The only clean thing she had was an oversized kid's jersey with "De Rosario 14" on the back. Perfect solution for covering up a naked toddler. With a few minutes to go, all the wives came down from the suite to field level. All Brandy was thinking was, "Don't you shit in my arms, boy."

It was extra special to have won this championship knowing they were in the stands. Of course, I didn't know what she had just gone through. I was on top of the world, and I wanted my boy to be on the field with me.

"Pass me Adisa!"

She shook her head no. What the hell?

"Hey! Pass me Adisa! I want to take him on the podium."

She waved me off. What was this woman's problem? I finally got to the railing where she was in the second row.

"Baby! C'mon, give me my boy!"

I'll never forget the look on her face.

"Okay. He doesn't have any bottoms on. Good luck."

I didn't have time to ask how that happened, but I knew it must have been hell. And there I was now, with him in my arms, being interviewed on national TV. All I was thinking was, "Boy, don't you pee on me on TV." Thank the Lord, he didn't.

Winning an MLS Cup our first year in our new home was incredible. To do it again the next year was more impressive. Again, Houston and New England were the two teams left standing. We were the champions, but everybody talked about us like the underdogs. Nobody thought New England would lose three finals in a row, and we didn't have our strongest team. Brian Ching and Ricardo Clark were out, leaving two big holes to fill. A lot of the weight fell on myself, Brad Davis, and Brian Mullan.

I didn't care who wasn't out there. I never once looked around and thought, "Ah, we don't have this guy. We don't have that guy." I was on the team, so we were winning. Call it cockiness, call it confidence; I don't really know what it is, but that was my mentality.

Before we left the locker room to take the field, I looked at myself in the mirror and reminded myself how I got there. I did that a lot. I was always the last guy out and didn't let anyone rush me. That was my time to separate myself. My moment to get in my zone. Then I would splash water on my face to get back to reality, run out to join my teammates in the tunnel, and tell 'em, "Yo! Let's do the business now!" I didn't care who was in my way. I was coming to dismantle them.

Whenever we would set up at the centre circle to start a game, I would squat down and look at my opposing defender right in the eye. If he looked away, I knew I was gonna kill him. If he looked back at me, I knew I was in for a long day. But I was ready for it. It was my way of seeing who was unsure, and I would attack them right away. I always wanted to find the weak link.

All 22 men on the field that day were up for the biggest fight of their careers. It was physical and intense right from the start. We didn't play well in that first half; we let New England dictate the game. Taylor Twellman scored 20 minutes in, and we were lucky to be down just 1–0 at halftime. I don't think I even sat down in the locker room. I started yelling before Dom could say anything. "We didn't come all this way to lose. We're the champions right now! Not them. They think they're going home with the trophy. Let's fucking go out there and take it from them again!"

Eleven pissed off men in orange took the field to start that second half. We were bringing the game to them now and had them on their back foot. We just needed to score a goal. We got lucky that Pat Noonan skied a shot over the net, which would have made it 2–0. I said to myself, "That's it. We're gonna change this game right now." We pushed the ball down field, and I took the defender all the way to the end line. With Brian injured, young Joseph Ngwenya started up front. I could see him at the top of the six-yard box. He was hungry, and I was ready to feed him. I played the ball across the face of the goal; he had two cracks at it and scored the tying goal. That changed the game. You could see the "Oh no, here we go again," look on all their faces.

A few minutes later, Brad Davis got the ball and gave me this look from 30 yards away: "Run." I sprinted towards the net, and he served up the perfect ball for me to head into the top corner: 2–1. I didn't get to do my shake 'n bake the year before. I made up for it at RFK. Our captain, Wade Barrett, was the first one over to me.

"Of course it was you! Big moment! Of course it was you!"

I loved the big stage. I wanted to win again more than anything. Now we just had to see out the last 15 minutes. The tables had flipped. They were desperate for a tying goal and threw everything at us. New England swung in a quick corner kick, and in all the commotion I lost my man. Jeff Larentowicz blew right past me. I don't even know how it happened. I never lost my man in the box. Of course, the ball fell right to him, and he got the perfect head on it. Luckily, Pat Onstad was my world-class goalkeeper. He made the save to bail us out. The last few minutes felt like forever.

It was such a relief when that final whistle blew. I couldn't believe it. I didn't know whether to yell and jump with happiness or fall over and cry. The bench was only feeling one emotion: pure joy. They came sprinting over to mob me. Rico rushed over with the biggest smile on his face. I knew he was heartbroken that he couldn't play, but he was so happy for me. We had made history. We were just the second team to win back-to-back MLS Cups.

It felt different than all the others. For the first time, I was present in everything that was going on. I could hear everything my teammates were saying to me and to each other. I could feel everyone's happiness. When I spotted Pat Onstad, I sprinted over to him. Pat and I were very close from all our time with the Canadian National Team. He knew how much this win meant to me, and I knew how much it meant to him. We had the biggest smiles on our faces, and we hugged each other, letting it all sink in. The emotions really swept over me then. Two Canadians on top of the American soccer world once more. That's all I was thinking about when they handed me the MVP trophy again. It wasn't just for me or my teammates. It was for Canada. MLS was changing, but our flag was planted.

CHAPTER 7

SHAKE 'N BAKE

When I watch my kids' soccer teams, it's easy to pick out the great ones from the rest. Most of these young kids are bold and try tricks they know may get them in trouble with their coaches. But if it works, their friends will be talking about it all week and put it on Instagram. But when the best player on the field still isn't satisfied after a special goal or a big win, that's how you know they've got a chance to make it.

It doesn't matter what level, the best want to play against the best. And when they've realized they're the best on that field, they want to play against even better teams, with even better players. It's this obsessive cycle, but all the greats feel that way from the first time they dominate a game until their playing days end. The last seven years of my career, the MLS All-Star Game was my annual chance to play against some of the best.

A lot of people criticize the MLS All-Star Game format, which sees the best MLS players face off against a European team that has come over on their pre-season tour. I don't understand why people who love soccer can see that as a negative. This is our chance to showcase our best against some of the biggest names in the game, and it allows us to test ourselves against players we may never get the chance to play against, or with, ever again. It mattered a lot to me to have that platform to showcase Canadian talent. A lot of these guys we were playing against had never even met a Canadian pro before. As a player, I loved that challenge. It's always an honour just to get a phone call to play in an All-Star Game and represent your league. Going up against these European giants is a commercial for our game.

In other sports, the All-Star Game is a break for a lot of guys. A chance to get together with friends who are your rivals all season. A chance to include your family in the festivities and, maybe, enjoy some quality time. And, of course, if you're not an All-Star, a chance to party during the season without consequences. But for me, the All-Star Game was the second-best thing to playing in the final: I got to test myself against some of the best players in the world.

In soccer we call an exhibition game a "friendly," which is ironic because in our game, there's no such thing as a friendly match when you put guys against each other who have something to prove. On their pre-season tour, a lot of these European guys are fighting for jobs, trying to justify why they deserve major minutes when their new season starts. Some of the MLS guys might be in the final year of their contract or are looking to make sure an All-Star Game appearance results in an even bigger one next time. Or maybe even a move overseas.

There is always so much to play for on both sides, which means the competition level is fierce. It's one of the only All-Star Games that is. The pressure is on these visiting teams; they're expected to wipe the floor with us. But the gap is not as wide as most of these Europeans believe, so MLS players are driven to prove they can compete. I like to think that for 90 minutes, most guys hated playing against me. These All-Star opponents must have hated me the most.

These were the games you had a completely different motivation for. Yes, I wanted the team to win. Yes, I was going to do everything to make my teammates look good. But it was my moment too. Everyone who didn't know my name was going to know who I was after those 90 minutes. I retired as the only MLS player to score or assist in every All-Star Game I played in. I live for the big moments.

People love to throw around that cliché, "You never forget your first." It's true.

My first All-Star Game was in 2006 when Chelsea came over to play the MLS All-Stars in Chicago. This was a big deal for the league. MLS wasn't star-studded like it is now. Remember, this was before David Beckham. There were plenty of stars in the league, and we knew how good we were, but MLS didn't get the attention it does now, at home or in Europe. The year before, they changed the format to invite a European club, and the MLS All-Stars embarrassed Fulham 4–1. A lot of people seemed surprised by that. I wasn't. Our league was getting better and better every year. Each crop of young guns was more impressive than the last. Clint Dempsey scored against Fulham in that game, and the next year Fulham bought him for a record $4 million transfer fee.

There was so much hype around this Chelsea game. I remember the media asking questions about it early in our season, like there was nothing else to talk about. Chelsea was one of the biggest clubs around: back-to-back Premier League champions, with one of the best managers in the world, José Mourinho. They were determined to stay on top in England and go farther in Europe than they ever had before. I was determined to show them that I could play against anybody. But with one of the richest owners in the game, Roman Abramovich, I wasn't playing against just anybody.

This was one of the most expensively assembled teams ever. I was up against John Terry, Ricardo Carvalho, Wayne Bridge, Michael Essien, Michael Ballack, Frank Lampard, Joe Cole, and Arjen Robben. All of these guys played in the World Cup in Germany just two months before. They were so loaded. I was excited to go up against those defenders. Again, you always want to test yourself against the best. Carvalho had won the UEFA Champions League with FC Porto and then followed Mourinho to Chelsea to win two Premier League titles. Terry was already being talked about as a future England captain and had a reputation for being one of the toughest guys to get around. But really, I was more concerned with Didier Drogba and Andriy Shevchenko.

They were two of the best goal scorers in the world. Chelsea had just paid £31 million to get Shevchenko from A.C. Milan that summer. Whatever Roman wanted, Roman got. When Chelsea bought Drogba for £24 million a couple of summers before, I remember thinking that would be the record transfer fee for a decade. Wrong. But transfer fees don't matter. There's always someone willing to sell you something for whatever amount they think you are crazy enough to write a check for. I wanted to see how I stacked up against these guys.

It felt like the longest All-Star week ever. Every day was jammed with media appearances and fan festivals. I loved all that, but I didn't want to talk about it anymore. I just really wanted to get out there and play these guys. Landon Donovan was the face of MLS but missed the game with an injury. I was ready to show everybody I was worthy of the same attention my old teammate was getting.

We had the field to practice on before Chelsea. I would quickly shower and then go back out to the touchline to watch them train. I spoke with a few guys. Michael Essien was a funny guy to talk to — that man was always in a good mood and trained like that kid who enjoys all the exhausting drills.

One day, Mourinho introduced himself to me with a smile. It felt cool that he knew who I was. I congratulated him on his success in England. He said he was going to keep a close eye on my right foot. Smart man.

It was exciting to know I was going up against one of the smartest guys in the game. People forget Mourinho was a player — because he wasn't a very good one. But he has this obsession for soccer that drives him. Any failure as a player was fuel to learn how to be the best manager. He learned from the very best and invented a new way of managing in a game that rarely reinvents itself.

There really is no one like him. Few people on the planet are as confident as Mourinho. It's easy to see how that makes so many people uncomfortable, and it's one of the reasons he's been so successful. You can feel when he walks into a room. When he talks to you, you listen. He wears his heart on his sleeve and when he knows he's right, he tells you. And he knows he's right a lot. The press loved and hated that, but they couldn't get enough of him then, and still can't. He had just shaved his head that summer. It was a really different look for one of the best-dressed guys in the game.

I watched Chelsea's training sessions closely. I wasn't spying on plays or studying their defenders. I wanted to see how they readied themselves. They were a championship team, at the peak of their powers. It was special, but I wasn't in awe. I was waiting for my chance to show these guys what I was all about. People would see me standing there and ask, "Dwayne, what are you thinking about?" I had the same answer every time.

"I'ma do the business."

We had a good team. The Dynamo were well represented in Chicago. Brian Ching, Ricardo Clark, and Eddie Robinson were there with me, and it was extra special for us to be there. The CONCACAF Champions League schedule didn't always allow for the best players to be there, or some guys needed the All-Star break to rest up. But the stars aligned for us that year.

Young Freddy Adu was on our team. He had just celebrated his 17th birthday, and here he was playing in his second All-Star Game, against the champions of England. I felt for the kid. Being the youngest professional athlete ever, there was so much pressure on him. The league wanted him to perform; the fans expected him to deliver. He played his first MLS game against my San Jose Earthquakes at 14 years old. Fourteen! Remember what I was doing when I was 14?

He didn't get to be a kid. Most kids are just starting high school at that age. He didn't get to live on his own or make mistakes. Adu was playing with men more than twice his age. And he was making more than 10 times what a lot of his teammates and most of the guys in the league were making back then. That $1 million Nike contract put a target on his back for sure. He hadn't proven himself in any major competitions. The powers that be were using him to get more attention for the sport. And all the power to Freddy. Soccer was what he knew, and soccer was what he loved. But I can't help but look where his career went and think, "Here's another example of a guy who got too much, too soon." I really hope he was able to soak in moments like that night in Chicago and enjoy himself throughout his career.

I must admit, I was envious of Freddy. He got to play with Jaime Moreno every day, one of my all-time favourite players. Moreno read the game like no one else. His movements off the ball and his vision made him an impossible player to mark. I remember our defenders in San Jose and Houston marking us differently in training before we would play D.C. United: sliding in quicker, leaning in with their hips earlier, trying to anticipate what it would be like to defend against Moreno on game day. None of that stuff worked. Moreno was so skilled and could read his opposition so well, it didn't matter if his defender was younger, faster, or stronger, he would adapt on the fly. Although I'm glad I never had to defend him for 90 minutes, I wish I could have played with him.

It was cool to stand with him in the tunnel at Chicago Fire's stadium, with Chelsea standing on the other side. In a way, it was like any other pre-game walk. You're focused. You're thinking about playing your own game. You glance over and size up the two centrebacks you're going to frustrate for 90 minutes. You feel like you're in that tunnel forever. There was a second, though, where Moreno and I both looked over at those blue shirts and had that, "Yo, we're playing Chelsea" moment. But when you walk out and take the field, you're just playing eleven guys that you are ready to show that you're better than. In front of twenty-one thousand people who probably don't think you are.

It's a really unique experience when you get thrown together with a bunch of guys you may have only played against a few times or only know because you disliked them for 90 minutes, and you had only a week to figure out how to win together before going up against a team of champions you've only ever watched on TV.

The game was so fast from the start. Jimmy Conrad made a hard tackle on Drogba a few minutes in. Jimmy wasn't afraid to be physical, and like the rest of us, he was ready to show what he was all about. Drogba didn't like it. He stood up with a mean-ass look on his face and said to Jimmy, "Hey. Me and you, not the same." I had to laugh. Didier was a beast on the field, and he wanted every player who went against him to know who they were dealing with.

I remember telling myself not to rush anything. Don't play any different than I would in any other game. Feel it out and wait for the moment. Make things simple, get myself into the game, and then start to express myself. I saw a chance to nutmeg Essien that I couldn't pass up. I saw the opening and just thought, "I'm taking this! Sorry, Mike." That's still a standout moment for me. It made for a great highlight on TV that night; I just wish I could've seen the expression on Essien's face as he turned around to chase after me.

Around the hour mark, I saw a chance to catch Chelsea sleeping on me. The more I drifted back into midfield, the more space they gave me. That was great when I had the ball and better when I didn't. We moved the ball through the halfway circle, and I started sprinting to split the two defenders. Alecko Eskandarian spotted my run and laid the ball off for me at the top of the box. I just needed one touch and I was going to blast it on net. But Geremi had me beat on the angle and knocked me over just as Alecko played it through for me. I knew my time was coming though. I could feel it.

Chelsea knocked the ball out of play and was trying to regroup as we set up for a throw in. Ronnie O'Brien picked up the ball and I ran towards him where there was all this space. He threw it right to me. It took a funny bounce though, and I couldn't play it with my left foot. I chipped it with my right foot so I could turn back to face the net. Jon Obi Mikel was the nearest blue shirt and came rushing in to mark me. I turned before he could get across me, but I couldn't get my full stride in. It left the ball right under me, and I knew if I tried to take another touch, he had all the momentum to kick it away before I got into the 18-yard box.

All of a sudden the net didn't feel 20 yards away. Adrenaline washed over me and took away any soreness I was feeling in my legs. Instinct took over. My hamstrings lit up and my mind yelled at me, "*Unleash this!*" I stepped into it and cracked it with my right foot. Top corner: 1–0 MLS.

What a feeling. To see the net bulge behind a sprawling Hilário. To see the crowd explode to their feet. To see O'Brien and Alecko yelling like kids as they ran over to congratulate me. That's when you can take it in. That's when you can celebrate, "I just scored a screamer against Chelsea in the All-Star Game!"

My shake 'n bake could've started an earthquake. People would always ask me, "Why do you do that when you score?" Because we all celebrated like that when we were kids. The shake 'n bake was my shoutout to all the talented kids I played with who didn't make it professionally. There are some goals you can't wait to get back and watch on video afterwards. That was one of them.

I was flying for those last 20 minutes. It's hard to describe the high you feel after hitting a ball like that, one that nobody saw coming. And against the two-time defending Premier League champions. I felt like one of those cartoon characters just bouncing up and down the pitch. Every stride felt longer than the last. I was ready to run my ass off until we could put our hands on that trophy. I was one of only four MLS guys to play all 90 minutes. Come on, how could coach Peter Nowak have taken me off after that goal?

When you get in your zone, there's no coming out. I wanted to win this game. I wanted to score another one so bad, I thought I blew my hamstring trying to outrun Geremi to a ball in their end. Thankfully, I didn't. But I had pushed myself as hard as I could, and my body was starting to fight back. My legs started cramping. I had put two games worth of miles on them at this point. The guys who chart the heat maps must've had an easy time marking up mine that night. Would have just been red everywhere, especially in those last few minutes.

Chelsea was throwing everything they had at us. The referee signalled for just two minutes of stoppage time. You could hear Mourinho loudly bossing his players from the dugout. It's incredible to hear all the different languages spoken on the pitch in one game. It was like a United Nations panic session out there. Mourinho was yelling in English and French, and even louder in Portuguese to Carvalho and Hilário. I wouldn't be surprised if he learned some Ukrainian when they signed Shevchenko. Mourinho had taken him off at halftime, but they had plenty of firepower.

Arjen Robben jumped three feet in the air to get his head on a ball that just went wide. John Terry was hungry for a goal. We turned the ball over at midfield and I noticed he wasn't in front of me. Somehow Terry had made his way up top. Frank Lampard spotted him and hit the perfect 20-yard pass. A lot of guys wouldn't be able to handle that pass. There was so much power behind it, but it was right on the money. Terry stretched out his right leg and deflected it across to Salomon Kalou at the top of the box. He settled it and got a good looking shot off, but there were too many red shirts in front of him. It was the best chance Chelsea had in a while but it went out for a throw in. Geremi threw the ball in, all the way to the middle of the box. We were all back defending and I was there to head it out for a corner kick.

Robben rushed over to take it and kicked the ball so quick, it sailed over everyone's head. It fell right in front of Carvalho at the far post, literally right on the edge of the six-yard box. He was in the perfect spot to score. You could tell Carvalho wasn't expecting the ball. And as a defender, he didn't think he was gonna be the guy in that spot to drive home the tying goal with his right foot. It surprised him that it had cleared all the red and blue shirts in front of him. Carvalho took one touch, then another to move it to his left foot, and hit it while falling down. That extra touch let goalkeeper Joe Cannon come out to cut down the angle and make a big save. It was so loud. Or maybe that was just the sound of relief in my head. I think I stopped breathing for a second when I saw the ball fall where it did. As a striker, you dream of those lucky bounces, and you bury those chances. Carvalho couldn't, and a few seconds later the referee blew the final whistle. We won.

We had beaten the back-to-back Premier League champions 1–0. For the second year in a row, MLS's best was better than a big-time team from London. So many people said we were gonna get smashed, that we didn't have any business playing on the same pitch as Chelsea. We showed them. We showed everybody. The world was looking at us now. The world was looking at me, a kid from Scarborough who was always being counted out. You couldn't have written the script any better. I scored the only goal to beat big-money Chelsea and walked away with the MVP trophy in my first All-Star Game.

That was special for everybody. All 18 players, the coaching staff, the league, the fans. You could see it on Jaime's face and mine when they presented the trophy. It always feels so long when you're up there. People have to make speeches and they have to do their thing for the cameras. We just wanted to put our hands on that trophy. Jaime was the captain and I was standing right next to him. You couldn't wipe the smiles off our faces as he lifted that trophy over his head, and we watched the crowd erupt.

My dad was in the stands with my brother. My wife was there with my kids. I had a few cousins and friends in town for the week too. It was one big family party — exactly what a moment like that should be. I was so happy they were all there to see that in the flesh. To see me shine on the big stage. Those are the moments you dream about sharing with the people you love the most. To do it feels almost surreal in the moment.

A few Chelsea players congratulated me on the field after. Michael Essien joked that he let me nutmeg him and said, "If somebody had to beat us, at least it was you." John Terry said I was a nightmare out there for him. My speed impressed him. I liked that. Drogba gave me props for my goal without even saying a word. It's cool when a guy doesn't have to say anything and can just give you a look.

Lampard was one of the first to come up to me. He complimented my game and said he was impressed with the show the league put on. That meant a lot. He was a fantastic player and one I really respected for how he carried himself on and off the field. I told him it was an honour to play him and said, "Maybe we'll play against each other again someday." I thought it would be in Europe, but I could tell he left that night with a real curiosity about this side of the world. I wasn't surprised when he signed with NYCFC. That's a man who has always thrived under the bright lights. That field might be small at Yankee Stadium, but the attention and experience Lampard got playing in MLS was huge. It's kind of wild to think back to playing against him in that All-Star Game, and thirteen years later he was managing Chelsea.

I was so full of confidence after that. It's one thing to know you belong. It's another thing to show it. I had the chance, and I did. When I was young, my Auntie Lea taught me, "You gotta get up and get." She was always teaching us proverbs and lessons we didn't understand at the time but grew up to value. I felt like these were the guys I should be playing against every week. Just like the kids I mentioned earlier, the best ones never lose that fire to want to play against the best. Sitting in the locker room after that game, I was dreaming about what it would be like to play in the Premier League. It kept my mind off my sore legs. The All-Star Game MVP trophy was pretty good ice though.

In 2012, I got the chance to play against Chelsea again, in what ended up being my last All-Star Game. Kind of funny how life works. This time Chelsea crossed the ocean as European champions. Winning the Champions League was the prize that Roman wanted the most, and the rare one that Mourinho couldn't deliver in his time there.

A lot of the same guys I played against six years earlier were still on the squad: Lampard, Terry, and Essien had a bit more swagger now that they were Champions League winners. And there were some new kids looking to prove themselves and maybe catch the attention of America at the same time. Eden Hazard, Romelu Lukaku, and Kevin De Bruyne got a run out in Philadelphia that day. If you told me at the time that only one of them would have success at Chelsea, I wouldn't have believed you.

I looked at this game as Chelsea's revenge game against me. But this time I had a few familiar faces standing next to me: Thierry Henry, David Beckham, and Landon Donovan were on the MLS team. That's part of what made it so special to be named team captain. Not only was I the first Canadian to wear the armband in an All-Star Game, but I was captaining three of the best players to have played in MLS. You would have thought one of them would be named captain.

Ben Olsen was the coach and my manager at D.C. United at the time. He pulled me aside and asked me how I would feel about captaining the team in Philly. I was totally taken aback. I was just happy to be on the team again and to have another crack at Chelsea in a big game. It really showed me the kind of guy Ben was: even with all that star power on the team, he respected me enough to give me that honour. It meant a lot. I really felt the appreciation that week from my teammates, the fans, and from the Chelsea guys who I had played against before. John Terry told me during the warm-ups, "Glad we're playing six years later because I know you don't have that pace anymore."

I just laughed at him. I knew I could still blow past him if I had the chance. But I was happy to see him get on the scoresheet in that game. I always respected him and how hard he worked on the pitch. I was much happier when Eddie Johnson scored the match winner for us in stoppage time, so I could say to J.T. at the end of the game, "Nice to beat you again. Mate!"

The All-Star Game in 2008 was a completely different story. It was in my city. The first MLS All-Star Game to be held outside of the United States. Now the league's showcase was on Canadian soil, and Toronto would get the spotlight it deserved.

With every Toronto FC game, the fans proved that the city was a soccer-smart market that was passionate about the sport and wanted to see the best. MLS was smart to not make Toronto wait long to host the summer showcase. How they chose West Ham United to be the All-Star opponent, I don't know. But it didn't matter that they weren't Premier League champions or playing in the Champions League. West Ham was a team full of hungry players looking to claim a spot on a team that was focused on growing a global brand. And that combination made them a great team to play against.

It was David Beckham's first MLS All-Star Game, which meant that he had all the attention leading up to the game, and that I felt I had to show him the best parts of *my* city. Again, Houston were MLS champions, and the All-Star Game fell at a weird time in the year for us, in the middle of a CONCACAF Champions League run. We had a couple of big games coming up and the Dynamo didn't want me to go. It might seem silly now, but back then it wasn't uncommon for star players to miss out on the All-Star Game because their club team needed them.

But I wasn't going to miss this game in my city. If I had two legs to run on, I was playing. There was nothing that was going to stop me. The

Dynamo tried, but if they really wanted me to miss out on the experience of playing in the league's showcase game in my hometown, they should have tried harder. I guess I can look back now and be thankful that they didn't.

Steve Nichol was head coach of the MLS All-Stars. He was also the manager of the New England Revolution, who we beat to win those back-to-back MLS Cups in Houston. When the team first got together at the hotel, he stuck out his hand, without a smile on his face, and said in the thickest Scottish accent, "Nice to have you on my team for once, so I can watch you kick someone else's ass."

Steve had a lot of respect for me as a player, and I had a ton of respect for him as a coach. Even more so after he told me that my coach Dominic had told him not to play me for more than 20 minutes.

"Fuck that, Steve! This is my All-Star Game, not Dom's. This is my city! My fans, my family — they're all here. I need to play 45 minutes."

I remember the look on his face. It was part "Damn, what am I supposed to do now?" and part "I'm glad he's not demanding to play all 90."

"What they said about you is true. When you say something, you mean it," he told me.

I'm glad that was the rep I had with other people. I had always been like that. My Auntie Lea used to always tell me, "Boy, you have too much of what the cat lick his ear with."

I know what you're thinking, "What the hell does that mean?" That was always our reaction the first time we heard one of Auntie's famous proverbs. They never made sense at first. Most of the time, we didn't really understand them until we grew up. This one was simple; it meant, "You talk too much. Hold your tongue." To this day I can still hear her saying that to me. But I believe I wouldn't have gotten certain things in my life if I was quieter or worried about what other people thought. Like what if I had told Steve, "Dom doesn't want me to play? Well, okay then." No way. I was never that kind of guy.

The first half of the game felt like three hours. I was itching, just waiting for the clock to tick faster so that I could get out there. We came out for the second half, and Steve hadn't put my number down to be substituted in. I thought, "Man, this guy better not put me in with five minutes to go." Eventually Steve told me to get warmed up. I sprang up out of my seat, and as soon as the crowd noticed, the whole stadium started cheering. I'd never had an audience for my warm-up stretches like that before.

Steve knew how to get the crowd up on its feet. He made a double substitution in the 59th minute, putting me in with Jimmy Brennan. That was the coolest experience. The crowd was so loud. If you were driving by the stadium, you would've thought that a goal had just been scored. To share that with Jimmy was special. I knew it meant a lot to Jimmy too, being the captain of Toronto FC and having a game like that on his turf.

I got stuck in right away. I had so much pent up energy sitting on the bench, waiting for my chance. And with the crowd behind me, I really felt good. I wanted to make sure they went home and had something to say about "that boy from Scarborough."

Juan Pablo Angel held the ball up in midfield, where I usually played. I sprinted by him and yelled for a pass. He hit it perfectly, playing me in past Australian captain, Lucas Neill. The one thing I knew about English soccer from watching Soccer Saturday with Graham Leggat was that those defenders love to dive in. So I dangled the ball like Thierry Henry used to do, looking to bait the defender. I cut into my left to take a shot, and Neill clipped me and took me down. It was the only way for him to stop me. Thankfully, the referee had the perfect view of it and pointed straight to the penalty spot. I didn't even have to say a word.

Usually when I got fouled, I didn't want to take the penalty shot. There was too much at stake, and if the foul was hard enough to leave me hurting, frustrated, or angry, I was in the wrong state of mind to take a penalty kick. But there was no way I was going to let someone else take that. It felt like the soccer gods were writing my script.

As I put the ball down on the spot and took my steps back, I said to myself, "There's no way I can miss a penalty in my hometown." I was determined to hit it as hard as I could into the corner. I could see in Rob Green's eyes, he had no idea what I was going to do. I hit it so hard, it nearly bounced out. It came crashing off the crossbar, straight down on the goal line, then bounced up off the bar and back down again. I was glad it happened in the south end, right in front of the most diehard fans. I shaked 'n baked all the way to the corner flag. Jimmy was the first teammate to come over to celebrate with me. It was a really special moment.

My goal turned out to be the winning goal. For the fourth year in a row, the MLS All-Stars had beaten a British team. Chicago's Cuauhtémoc Blanco was named MVP, and it was cool to get to know him a little bit that week. I had only had a few exchanges with him on the field before that week in Toronto. Same with David Beckham. That's the bonus with these All-Star Games: you get to spend some time with guys you probably wouldn't get the chance to otherwise.

The leagues always throw a party for their sponsors and partners to mingle and meet with players and those involved in the game. And when you're in a different city, like during All-Star week, players want to experience the city in a genuine way and hang out with the locals. You don't really get that chance during the season. I had a responsibility to show off the very best of my city. I've always been about bringing people together.

My brothers and I started a company, DeRo Entertainment. That 2008 All-Star post-game party was our first event. We rented a couple of levels at one of the most popular clubs downtown, known as Century Room at the time. It was the party of the summer. And that's no disrespect to Caribana. Kevin Hart was there. We hired Estelle to do a special performance for the crowd, and everyone got a gift bag with David Beckham's cologne in it. We had a bunch of local celebrities in the house too. There was a whole Hollywood vibe going on, just as an All-Star party should feel. I think that might have surprised David Beckham. I expected him to come by for a little bit, but I knew he was being pulled in a hundred different directions. I guess I shouldn't have been surprised that he enjoyed our party and the music so much, he stayed with us. Beckham was jamming to the hip-hop and the reggae like the rest of us. He's a real down to earth guy who just wanted to have a good time like everybody else. Plus, anyone who has partied in Toronto before knows that our music mix is the best. Everybody on the team came out, and it turned out to be a big night. It showed me how many people really had respect for me and for my city.

At the end of the day, I lost quite a bit of money putting that on. My brother did all the catering for the event, and he took the biggest hit that night. But the money didn't matter. I wanted to give the people in my sport the best experience possible, and I wanted to show my city how big the game could be and how big the party could be when you did it right. People still talk about that party to this day. It was a really cool night.

Dominic Kinnear wasn't happy when I got back to Houston. He was one of the first guys I saw on my first day back at training. No smile, no hello, no "How was it?" Just, "You better fucking help us win this weekend."

CHAPTER 8

DER-O CANADA

My parents came to Canada with so little. Not a day goes by that I'm not thankful they planted roots in Canada. I'm thankful my children have had the chance to live and go to great schools here. I've always had such a deep sense of pride for my country. It didn't matter what I went through growing up or what problems I saw on the streets. Canada was the place for me. It means the world to me that I got to wear the red and white Canada crest over my heart. They were some of the most challenging times of my life, but playing for my country is something I'm so very proud of.

I wanted nothing more than to play for my country in a World Cup. Yes, it's every young soccer player's dream. But when you get so close to achieving it and it doesn't come to fruition, it's heartbreaking. In a country this great, Canada has only reached one World Cup — in 1986 — and all I remember is them finishing last and not even scoring a goal. Still, some of the best moments of my life came while playing for Canada.

To this day, people come up to me to talk about Canada's CONCACAF Gold Cup win in 2000 — our one and only regional championship. They're so excited. They tell me where they watched the game and who their favourite players were. I've met quite a few kids born in 2000 or 2001 named Carlo or Craig. It's special to see how much it meant to some people. For many, it's the proudest they've been as Canadian soccer fans. It was such a big moment for Canadian soccer — and we almost didn't play.

I played 81 games for the Canadian National Team in my career. Bob Lenarduzzi gave me my first international call-up in 1997. It was something I had dreamed about and worked so hard for. It was an incredible moment for me and my family. I probably slept for just two hours that night. I bet you my dad didn't sleep at all, he was so excited. Bob called Paul Stalteri and me in to the team after we both had great tournaments in Malaysia at the U-20 World Cup. It was a cool experience to be the youngest guy in Bob's senior team camp, even though I didn't play in that first match.

Paul, Jason Bent, Robbie Aristodemo, and I were the four new guys from Ontario to really look out for. To me, we were just four guys who were relentless and wanted to make it. There were a lot of other guys I played with while growing up that were good enough to have been there with me, but for one reason or another, they never got to live that dream. I was aware of how blessed I was to get to. I only saw things through the eyes of a Scarborough kid. But when I started to play in Edmonton, Vancouver, and the States, and watched guys play with passion in that national team shirt, it opened my eyes to what it meant to be a Canadian international player.

I was watching the national team for a few years and thought, "Man, they need a player like me. A player that can play and knock ball with the Mexicans and Central Americans and play their style of football. But better."

I've got to give a lot of credit to Alex Bunbury, Randy Samuel, and Kevin Holness. These guys really took me under their wing. They were all West Indian too. They understood me and made me feel like one of the guys. They'd bring me out to dinner and invite me over to their houses. Randy and Kevin really encouraged me. They took to me and wanted to make sure I realized the potential they saw in me. Randy, especially, would go out of his way to make sure I was comfortable.

"You really have something special. DeRo, you're gonna change the game for Canada," Randy told me.

I was fearless. In one of my first national team camps in Vancouver, we split the squad up and played a full-sized game against each other. Paul Dolan was in net for the other side. He loved to wander around the box and was always off his line. I got the ball at the centre circle and thought, "I'm just gonna chip this guy." I hit the ball as hard as I could and put it right over his head into the back of the net. He couldn't believe it. Neither could anybody else out there that day. That's ballsy. But I was that guy. I'm street. Every chance I got, I thought, "I'm gonna make you know my name." If I had five minutes on the pitch with the national team, I was gonna take that opportunity. I have to give my dad a lot of credit for that mentality. He really instilled that in me.

"I don't care if they give you five minutes or two minutes or 10 seconds on the pitch. You make the best of the time they give you."

Getting the call-up to the national team for the 2000 CONCACAF Gold Cup was such a huge moment. After what had happened in Germany and where I was in my career with the Richmond Kickers, playing in the Gold Cup was a massive opportunity for me. I wanted to take that step up, and this tournament provided the stage for me to get noticed by MLS teams. I also understood that I was a young guy on the team who had to prove his worth. We had guys on the team who played in Europe and all over the world. There was a strong balance of young guys and proven veterans. I knew it was going to be a tough lineup to crack, and it was. But I was excited to be in that environment and learn from some really experienced players that I respected. And I was thankful Holger Osieck, who took over as head coach when Bob stepped down in 1998, saw my value and gave me the chance.

"You do some surprising things. You have a great energy and work really hard for this team. You're going to be very valuable to us going forward," Holger told me.

We had a really strong training camp in L.A. The sessions were hard, and the guys really pushed each other. We were well prepared for a long run in the tournament. Throughout that camp though, the senior players were continuing to negotiate with the Canadian Soccer Association over our payment and bonus structure. The back and forth was intense and went longer than either side wanted. It was getting to crunch time, but you never would've known based on how well we practised and bonded on the field.

After one session, some of the veterans pulled all the young guys aside and explained how bad things were. Jeff Clarke, Richard Hastings, Jimmy Brennan, and I just sat there in shock. They explained how frustrated they were with the back and forth with the CSA. It was hard to believe. There was no bonus structure, and the contracts weren't incentivized in the ways they were for other countries. Frustrated in one of the negotiation sessions, someone from the CSA had told the players group, "You guys aren't going to win this tournament, so why do we need to put an incentive clause in here for that?"

The overall terms just weren't fair. I wasn't involved, but I knew enough about contracts at the time to know that they were trying to take us for a ride. The veteran guys felt like they were all out of options. "We're going to strike unless they agree to improve these terms."

We were just young guys, getting our first real taste of international soccer. We weren't really in a position to say no. But we fully supported the veterans. We knew that what they were fighting for would benefit everybody and set a precedent for the future.

I did worry, though. What if this didn't work out? I was trying to establish myself on the national team. What if I was blacklisted and didn't get any more opportunities after this? But I knew that was how everybody in the situation felt.

"If that's how you guys feel and you want to strike, we're with you. We're a team," we told them.

It put Holger in a really tough situation. It must have been a horrible balancing act for him. He was contracted to work for the CSA, but he couldn't coach if his players wouldn't play. Our first game was in two days and there was no agreement. Holger told us, "Obviously, I'm stuck between two rocks here. But you guys do what you need to do. I hope that means you'll be out there on the field playing for me and your country."

One of the executives came down and gave a speech to the room. He didn't know our names. That showed me how little respect the CSA had for our team, which just brought us closer together. We all agreed that the terms just weren't good enough. We told him where we stood, and we weren't going to budge until they treated us like a valued part of Canadian Soccer.

Everyone in that room loved wearing that shirt and was so proud to represent our country. But we weren't going to be taken advantage of. And we weren't asking for the world.

It came down to the wire. They finally came to an agreement the day before our first game. The CSA was not happy at all, but our team was solidified as a unit after that experience. We had shown each other that we had each other's backs. We were willing to walk out and not play because we believed in what we were fighting for. As a Canadian team, we stuck together and were willing to face the consequences. I really feel in my heart that's why we won the Gold Cup. That's how we were able to beat Mexico and Colombia and other top teams. We believed in ourselves. I'd never seen Canada play with that belief before. We also had a lot of good fortune on our side.

There really was something magical about that 2000 Gold Cup. There was this snowball effect of good luck. We could do no wrong on the field. If we were down, we'd find a way back. The balls bounced our way. And so did the coins. In 2026, when the FIFA World Cup expands to 48 teams, a lot of people are going to have a hard time accepting three-team groups.

The 2000 Gold Cup was a 12-team tournament. To make up four groups of three, CONCACAF invited Colombia, Peru, and South Korea to play. We were drawn into Group D with Costa Rica and the Koreans. We tied our first game against Costa Rica in San Diego. They scored early and then forward Carlo Corazzin scored from a penalty just a few minutes later. Costa Rica took the lead early into the second half, and Carlo scored for us again to tie it up just a few minutes later. Two days later we tied South Korea 0–0 at the Coliseum in L.A. Then they tied Costa Rica 2–2 to wrap up the group, leaving us all tied on two points. Because they had scored four goals, Costa Rica won the group, as expected. We were tied with South Korea in every category, which meant the advancing team was decided by a coin toss. Could you imagine that today?

Lots of people think penalty shootouts are an unfair way to decide a winner. A coin toss left it all to the gods. It might sound crazy, but I didn't have any doubt that we were going to win that toss. Everybody felt like it was going to go our way. Our coach went into a media tent with the Korean coach and the official flipped a coin. The coin went up, fell, then Holger turned around and gave a thumbs up. We were through to the knockout stage for the first time ever.

Nobody gave us a chance to beat Mexico. They were the 10th ranked team in the world at the time. Canada was 85th. In 20 games against El Tri before that quarter-final, Canada had won twice. Mexico had Rafa Márquez, Claudio Suárez, Gerardo Torrado, Ramón Ramírez, and Luis Hernández. But we had Craig Forrest and Carlo Corazzin.

Carlo worked so hard in training. You knew good things were going to happen for him because of how hard he worked. He knew he might not be the most skilled player on the field, but he was definitely going to work the hardest. During the game against Mexico, Rafa Márquez kicked Carlo so hard in the nuts as they jumped for a header. I didn't think he was going to stand up again. Alex McKechnie, the team physiotherapist, rushed out to help Carlo and came back to tell the bench, in the thickest Scottish accent, "He's not having children."

Somehow, Márquez didn't get booked, and Carlo was able to shake it off and stay in the match. With less than 10 minutes to play, Martin Nash whipped a perfect ball in for Carlo to head past Mexican goalkeeper Óscar Pérez. We were tied. The Mexicans didn't know what had hit them. Extra time was sudden death, and we launched a quick attack. Martin picked out Richard Hastings sprinting towards the net, and he roofed it past Pérez. Little Canada had beaten mighty Mexico, 2–1! It was the greatest Gold Cup upset ever.

We all exploded off the bench and ran towards Richard. I was so happy for him. We had played together on the U-20 team. I had never seen him play with that level of confidence and energy, to take over a match like that. While we were celebrating on the field, trying to process what just happened, I turned around to look at the stands. They were empty. All those green shirts had vanished. You could hear the person yelling from row 50: "Way to go, eh?"

It felt like there were 10 people in the stands for our semifinal against Trinidad and Tobago. The Coliseum held ninety-three thousand, and there weren't even three thousand people in there that night. Dwight Yorke was a star at Manchester United. He didn't play in that match, though T&T were still the favourites. But we had just beaten Mexico. We were really starting to believe this was our tournament to win. Craig stood on his head in net. He stopped a penalty shot in the first half, and T&T just couldn't do anything to put a shot past him. Defender Mark Watson scored the game's only goal to put us through to the final against Colombia.

The vibe and the energy on the team was electric. Everyone was contributing. We had no flaws. Everyone who got on the field played some of the best games of their careers. We were relentless, and we wanted to put our hands on that giant trophy. Only Mexico and the United States had won the Gold Cup. We wanted to be on that list.

I wonder what the Colombians were thinking on the bus ride to the stadium the morning of the final. There was a lot of pride in that Colombian team, and they were working to rebuild their reputation after struggling at the 1994 World Cup in the U.S. And while they definitely showed up to battle, this wasn't their confederation's tournament. On the other hand, we knew this was our moment to plant a flag for Canadian soccer. Jason de Vos scored to give us the lead just before halftime, and Carlo scored a penalty in the second half. There was no way back for the Colombians. I couldn't sit still on the bench. I was begging the clock to tick by faster and faster. Finally, the referee blew his whistle and we stormed the field to celebrate.

It was amazing for us, and for Canadian soccer. Finally, there was something other than making the 1986 World Cup to talk about. Nobody thought we could do it. Even on the podium, FIFA vice-president Jack Warner looked disappointed. He must have thought his home country of Trinidad and Tobago was going to be on the podium instead. When you play for Canada, you quickly realize there are dark forces against you. The officials don't always have your back, and it feels like the Confederation doesn't want you to succeed at the expense of the giants, USA or Mexico. In Central America, the fans intimidate the referees in ways you just don't see in North America. The most mind-blowing refereeing decisions you can imagine happened against us in CONCACAF. All the time.

After winning the Gold Cup, I thought things would be different when Canada played. Trinidad and Tobago and Mexico got their revenge a few months later, beating us in World Cup qualifiers and crushing our dreams of playing at the 2002 World Cup. As Confederation champions, we did go to Japan for the 2001 Confederations Cup, which was an incredible experience for all of us on the team. We lost to Japan and Cameroon, but we tied Brazil, the eventual World Cup winners. That left us on such a high. But flying home, it was so disappointing to know that we wouldn't be returning the next year to play in the World Cup.

Canada has been starved of soccer success for so long. There's a real hunger right now, not just from the fans and this new crop of players, but from everyone in this country who loves the game. Victor Montagliani, the president of CONCACAF, is Canadian, and that should help the national program at all levels, on and off the field.

There's something special happening right now. There's a hope and a belief amongst the national team that wasn't always there. John Herdman deserves a lot of credit for that. First with his work in the women's game and now with the men's Canadian National Team, he has shown what it's like for a team to have an identity. He's taught his teams how important it is to play for the player beside you at all costs and to enjoy the success that comes along with it, but to also use it as motivation to work harder and achieve even more. Not every unit was able to fully buy into that in the past.

———

We won two championships and created such a winning culture in San Jose. When Frank Yallop left, it was Dominic's time to shine. And when Landon left, it was my turn. There was this constant belief that we were going to win. We felt unstoppable, and there was never a doubt in any game or any league that we weren't going to win. We always had that strong belief in ourselves and in our abilities, and we were all on the same page. To be honest, I didn't realize how unique that was.

I never had the same feeling with the national team or anywhere else I played. I tried my best to recreate that environment, but it was really hard. As a player, you can only do so much to motivate others, whether that's showing up earlier, staying later, or working harder in the gym.

In San Jose and Houston, we weren't angry when we lost a match. We were disappointed because we knew some way, somehow, we should've gotten back in the game. It was infectious. We had the mentality, "Let's take the game to them. Let's show them what we're made of." We never went to Mexico and thought, "Pachuca. Club America. These environments are tough." We didn't just want to compete. We played our game, we pressured them. We didn't just sit back. It was a back and forth battle. We got a lot of respect from those teams because of that.

Frank tried to bring that mentality to the Canadian National Team. I don't think he had the right support. He tried to get us more games at home and against stronger competition. I understood it because I had won. Not many guys on the national team had won before. It's hard to teach that mentality when you doubt yourself, your team, and your country.

Every time we played a stronger team away, our mentality became: "Try not to get scored on first." How about, let's score first. Let's just play. We're the underdog, we all know that. Just go out there and play your ass off. Take shots from outside the box. It's okay if you lose the ball. Get it back. Run at defenders. Take guys on. Don't hold back, and play with confidence. Just see what happens.

We always had this fear that it would collapse. One thing might go wrong, and then confidence would slide. And once that happened, players would be afraid to play through the seams, which would affect results. Frank wanted a more proactive team — one that was willing to go anywhere and dictate the tempo and the pace. Or die trying. It didn't matter if it was Mexico, or Honduras, or Guadeloupe.

Obviously, there are times you have to adapt that philosophy. In those environments fear and self-doubt only feeds the beast more. The "Olés" come out, and you're looking at 11 Lionel Messis out there. Their lowest point is when you're taking the game to them and their fans turn on them. Look for that the next time you're watching a Central or South American team. It really affects them negatively. There were very few times we were able to do that. It was frustrating.

In soccer, you have to work with what you got. And Canada just hasn't had a game-changing forward who can turn a match around or create chance after chance. Alphonso Davies could be that guy. Jonathan David could be that guy. That player could be developing in the Toronto, Vancouver, or Montreal academy right now and could really make his mark when Canada co-hosts the World Cup. I'm happy for the group that will represent Canada in 2026, on so many levels. But for one, I'm very happy that they won't have to go through the stress of World Cup qualifiers.

At the start of every World Cup qualifying cycle, I believed we were going to get through. That's how you have to think if you're going to win. Not every Canadian thinks that way.

———

I've always felt this special connection to Africa. The continent has such an incredible history and spirit. Growing up in Scarborough, I was always around African cultures and beliefs. I studied Haile Selassie. I read a lot of books about him, and his beliefs and messages resonated with me. I liked the history and learning about the conflicts and enemies he fought both from outside and within. When it was announced that South Africa would host the 2010 World Cup, the first on that continent, it was a victory for all of Africa. I really wanted it to be my first World Cup too.

Dale Mitchell was Canada's coach for that 2010 qualifying cycle. His approach was very defensive minded, which really disappointed me because he was a striker. He scored a record 19 goals for the national team. I broke that record in the next World Cup qualifying cycle. Maybe I could've gotten there sooner. At the time, I wasn't thinking about it at all. But I knew that as a team, we were capable of so much more.

I wanted us to start thinking like a proactive team instead of a reactive team. We had the pieces to do that, but we never really took the game to our opponents. We always sat back, held the shape, and tried to surprise them on the counterattack. I never liked that approach, especially when we were at home. We gave our opponents the chance to play their game and build momentum, leaving us on our back foot. We were set up as a conservative, counterattacking team.

We were expected to get through our semifinal group, but we made a mess of it from the start. We tied Jamaica in Toronto in our first game and then lost to Honduras in Montreal. I remember feeling like the football gods were against us that night at Saputo Stadium. The field was all torn up, and the ball was bouncing all over the place. And it felt like a home game for Honduras, which it always did when they came up to play us because thousands of Honduran Americans would drive up from New York and pack the stadium in blue.

We did score first, thanks to Adrian Serioux. It was the only goal he ever scored for the national team. Patrice Bernier swung in the perfect corner kick, and Adrian headed the ball past the keeper. It was definitely the start we needed. A few minutes later, Tomasz Radzinski almost doubled our lead, but he couldn't get his best shot off because the Honduran defender bodychecked him like a hockey player into the ad boards. Tomasz had cut up his fingers and had to leave the game. The referee didn't even call a foul. What country doesn't get that call in their favour when they're playing at home? Us.

We played with 10 men for seven minutes before they could get his replacement on. That was such a big loss for us. Tomasz was a very good player and made life very difficult for every defender he played against. People seem to forget, Tomasz had a great career in England with Everton and then Fulham. He was a very special player to the national team, and we really missed him out there that night.

We had our chances, though. I was played in on a breakaway but the linesman put the flag up for offside. I didn't think it was, but no goal scorer ever does. Then Ali Gerba headed one off the post at the end of the first half. A 2–0 lead would've changed everything for us. Instead, Honduras took all the momentum from our missed chances and from the crowd cheering them on because there were way more Honduran fans than Canadian. They scored two quick goals, and we just couldn't get anything going. Then Bernier was shown a red card, and we spent the rest of the match feeling like we'd never get a fair call. Sadly, a lot of games felt like that.

It eventually became a guarantee. Wake up in the morning, go to the match, lace up your boots, take the field, and never see the calls go your way. We never got any favours. Like I said, it felt like there was an outside force that didn't want Canada to succeed. We never got the calls; we never got those lucky bounces. Home or away. Every 50-50 call went against us. That's how all the players felt. That's a tough reality to face, especially if you're coming from a successful club team or an environment where winning doesn't feel like such a challenge.

I would like to be the national team coach one day. I'm the only player who has been through all phases of the national program since Bob Lenarduzzi. I have a grasp and understanding of what it takes to compete and what it takes to be successful in CONCACAF. There are so many elements to playing international soccer in this region; it's unlike any other place. A lot of it is psychological, but the only person who proposed working on the mental side of our game when I was involved in the program was René Simões. He didn't get the national team head-coaching job in 2007, but I was in the room when he pitched his plan to the board of governors and I thought, "This guy gets it."

You have to be able to manage individuals. That's just as important as preparing the players physically for the match and task at hand. In Canada, there are a lot of players who come into a national team camp with low self-confidence because they're not getting many minutes or much opportunity with their club team. You've got to make that player feel important, so he delivers in your camp. I know John Herdman has put a major focus on that now and is developing a real identity within the national program.

Canada lacks a soccer identity. Every other soccer nation has one. And it can evolve and change. Look at how quickly the Americans evolved to a more skilled game. And now that a lot of those players have moved on, like Landon, DaMarcus Beasley, Oguchi Onyewu, U.S. Soccer is working to find a new identity. Structure is very important with a national team because you just don't have the guys together for very long. How they're going to play and set up offensively and defensively have to be drilled in with every camp.

When Benito Floro first came on board, his main focus was on set pieces. We ran so many throw in drills, and some days we would spend the entire session just working on corner kicks. He'd make me hit 20 free kicks in a row from the same area, just so we could work on something he saw. According to his research, the percentage of goals from dead ball situations was so high that it would be the key to winning games in these countries and atmospheres where we struggled in the past. We had set plays for absolutely everything, which I thought was very cool.

I had a really good relationship with Benito. He had seen the entire spectrum of soccer and had dealt with every type of player and every type of situation. His book could be a thousand pages long. But he couldn't take the pieces he had and qualify for a World Cup, so his time in charge was short. That's how the business goes.

—

There's nothing quite like international football. You get to see the world, and you get to play with your countrymen who you may see only a couple of times a year, when the national team gets together for a camp. Nothing brings the team together like travelling with the group. Not the actual flight, because you're probably spread out throughout the plane with everybody else. Maybe you're sitting next to fans who are going down for the game or Canadians who are visiting family or headed south for a sunny vacation. Imagine their surprise when they find out they're sitting next to a professional footballer. That was always a fun conversation.

"Hey there, fella. What brings you down to Costa Rica?"

"Soccer. I'm a professional footballer. We're with the national team and we're playing Costa Rica in a couple of nights."

"What? Get outta here. No really, what are you getting up to in Costa Rica? Are you going down for the fitness conference out in the jungle?"

It isn't as funny when you're flying to Europe for a game. Europeans already think Canadian soccer is a joke because we fail to qualify for every World Cup. Imagine when they realize they're sitting next to stars of the team on a discount red-eye flight. That's not professional. That's not right.

It's 2021, and we still don't have a national training centre, where players can stay and train, and use top-class facilities. And we want success? And we expect to make a World Cup? I played with three generations of players on the national team. I was in camps with Alex Bunbury, Randy Samuel, and Paul Peschisolido. Craig, Carlo, and Jason de Vos were stars on our Gold Cup winning team — Craig won Most Valuable Player and Carlo was the leading goal scorer that tournament. Jimmy Brennan, Atiba Hutchinson, Julian de Guzman, and I were all on the squad in our primes. I played with Jonathan Osorio and Cyle Larin from this new crop, who have everyone hopeful for the future.

It's incredible to step back and look at all the players who have played in the national team set-up. The one constant? The way everything is organized. All this time has passed, but it operates the same way. Alex, Craig, Jimmy, and Oso all have the same stories. Generations have passed, and yet the experience hasn't evolved. Nothing has grown. We had to wait for America to expand their league north of the border and occasionally sell out BMO and Saputo and BC Place before Canadians realized, "Wow, a lot of people really like soccer up here." Yeah, no shit.

I read a newspaper article after Toronto FC's first home game. The team brass was shocked they sold out. They're just business people; they didn't tap into the DNA of the football community. While they may have tapped into a portion of the community — the British — they didn't take into account the Caribbeans, Croatians, Italians, and Portuguese, who had been waiting for something bigger. There was nothing that could bring these groups together. But that was what Toronto FC did. It brought everyone out organically because all these communities had been craving something like this. But it's not completely ours.

Developing Canadian players wasn't important to Toronto FC, the Vancouver Whitecaps, and the Montreal Impact for a long time. That's what makes the Canadian Premier League so important. It is 100 percent Canada's league, for Canadians. I know there are some foreign players in the league, but they're helping develop and improve the quality of our players. If you don't give someone a platform to try and succeed, you'll never know.

In Canada we have our own papers, our own stations, but too often it seems like local content isn't interesting enough to have airtime or print space. It will never grow if we bury it and don't push it. Jamaica has its own pro league. Their track and field program develops world-class athletes. They support their own and sell out stadiums at youth level. That doesn't happen here. We can't get people into smaller arenas to support the best Canadian university talent. But people will pay $200 to $300 for one ticket to a regular season hockey game. Obviously there are a lot of factors at play, but from an organizational perspective, we can definitely start by establishing an environment where players want to be there and be a part of something special.

When people ask me, "How can Jonathan de Guzman choose to play for Holland instead of Canada? How come Owen Hargreaves got his British citizenship and didn't play for the country he was born in?" I give the same answer every time: "Because we make it easy for them."

Jono went to the Netherlands at a very young age and has lived there for a long time. If we had made him feel like, "Jono we miss you. You're Canadian. This is where you belong. We really want you," he probably would've considered it. But we didn't and we don't. And I'm not talking about fans. We don't get enough support at the corporate level or at the governing body level. You always hear, "We don't have enough this; we don't have enough that." That's just bad management. Every time a player is involved with a national camp, they should get something more than a little plaque. The sponsors should be taking care of the players. The federation has a responsibility to give these players incentives to want to play for their national team. And the result would be a better environment to develop these players.

When you come into a national team camp and the equipment guy says, "Hey, after the game we need these jerseys back because we're giving them to the youth team," it feels so amateur. They're paid professionals. These guys are leaving their families, leaving their jobs, leaving their positions on their club teams, putting their careers at risk, and they can't even go home with their shirt? An international cap is a really proud moment for any player. That's a memento you want. One you cherish.

You never know how many caps you're going to get. I was very blessed to get 81. I won the Canadian Player of the Year award four times, and what they'd give me? What recognition did I get? First time I won, Frank Yallop went out of his way to get me an autographed Pelé jersey. He did that on his own because that's the kind of guy Frank is. He knew how hard I worked and how dedicated I was to the craft, no matter how successful the team was or how well I played. After my second POTY award, I got a Sony gift card from the CSA. I didn't even know how much it was for. I went into the Sony store at Scarborough Town Centre, and one of the boys I grew up with was working there. He swiped the card and said, "Yo, you were Player of the Year . . . and they gave you a $500 gift card?"

American guys are getting Rolex watches or cars. I would lie to people about what I got because I was embarrassed — not for myself, but for Canada.

We don't need big budgets to make guys feel special. When you provide more incentive, guys commit harder. There's more drive. There are so many little things that are overlooked, but doing them would make such a big difference and help the sport on so many levels. Put guys on TV. Celebrate Canadian players who succeed on their club team — whether they're playing in MLS or in Turkey or in China. Maybe guys playing in Europe wouldn't decline a national team invite and would put up with the travel if there was an incentive to play that friendly in Costa Rica. I understand why Steve Nash stopped playing for the national basketball team when he did. Why would he leave what he was doing in Phoenix and risk his body when we treat our national sports programs like a joke operation?

When I retired from the national team, they brought me out before a game and I waved to the stands for two seconds before disappearing into the abyss. There might have been two thousand people in the crowd. It felt cheap. It made me feel like all those years I spent with the program and all those sacrifices I made weren't really appreciated. I always took the call when it came from the national team. I never turned down an opportunity to play for my country. It just didn't feel like the right way to end it. But then again, I didn't get to leave the field wearing a Canadian shirt the way that I wanted to.

CHAPTER 9

HOMECOMING

There's no place like home.

No matter where you're from or when you grew up, it's a phrase we've all heard. It doesn't matter where home is, how big it is, or even if you like it. *There is no place like home.*

Scarborough is my soul. The culture is in my blood. The people have always been on my mind. The hood where I grew up is just one part of Scarborough. Scarborough is just one part of Toronto. Toronto is just one part of Canada. And there's no place like Toronto.

It took a long time for the world to realize Toronto's greatness. I always got a different reaction when I would tell people where I was from. Some would be wide-eyed and excited. Some people didn't have a clue. Some snickered because they were jealous. Others asked if I knew some random person they knew. And there were always a few who asked, "Okay, cool, what state is that in?"

Whatever you want, Toronto's got it. Every part of the world has their own corner in Toronto. You want to eat Ethiopian tonight? Here are 10 spots. You want to find a DJ playing UK garage music on Friday?

Pick one of these three. Toronto has got it all. But for the longest time, it didn't have a Major League Soccer team.

In 2005, MLS awarded Maple Leaf Sports & Entertainment an expansion franchise. It cost MLSE $10 million. I wish I could have bought a club back then. By 2019, the expansion fee had gone up to $200 million. For years I heard, "Soccer will never be a big deal in North America." Look at it now.

For me, there was a new dream. I didn't know when. I didn't know how. But I knew I had to play for my hometown club.

For weeks, my phone blew up with the same text message: "When you coming home, DeRo?"

Every time I read about the plans for the club, it tugged on my heart. When they chose the name "Toronto Football Club," I was proud. A bold, strong, traditional name that put the city first. My city.

For years, I watched other places try names that appealed to the general American sports fan. While those names might have had some history and meaning to those cities, they didn't sound like a soccer team. Past Toronto teams tried to appeal to specific communities. Toronto Metros-Croatia won the NASL's Soccer Bowl in 1976, led by the late Eusébio.

Toronto FC. TFC. That was different. That was classic. That was for everybody in, and from, Toronto.

When they unveiled red as the club colour, it was almost too perfect. Canada's first team in America's soccer league had to be red! The thought of 10 players in red shirts, shorts, and socks on a pitch in Toronto that they could call their own every matchday got me excited on so many levels. I was excited for my city and my community, which had been waiting for a club to represent them on a big soccer stage. I was excited for Canadian kids who could grow up watching a team that was their own, with Canadian players. One day, one of those players could be them.

I had been away for 13 years. I missed Toronto. I couldn't wait for my wife and kids to fall in love with the hometown I was always talking about. The city had changed so much. The old Toronto couldn't fill a 20,000-seat stadium week in and week out. This Toronto quickly showed the world what an incredible fan base was waiting for a team to call their own.

I'll never forget watching SportsCenter the day Danny Dichio scored the first goal in club history. I don't even remember the goal. All I can picture are the seat cushions raining down on the greenest turf in the world. Twenty thousand people in the stadium. Twenty thousand seat cushions thrown as high and as far as possible. I could feel the emotions of my city: the joy of having a goal to celebrate; the relief of that first goal, after four goalless games. I wanted that experience. I needed that experience.

As if the football gods had planned it, my first game at BMO Field was the week after the cushion-toss game. Toronto FC versus Houston Dynamo. It was the first fixture I circled when our schedule came out. My Houston teammates joked that they needed tickets for so-and-so or some made-up relative. I was Mr. Ticketmaster. The clubs knew how important that first match was for me, and they were great. They gave me about 80 tickets for my family and friends, and I bought another hundred tickets for anyone else who wanted to be there to see me. It felt really special to have my own section, in my city. And Toronto FC could see the impact I had. The people at the top at the time really weren't soccer people, they were businessmen. When they saw the support I had, that's when the light bulb went off.

After my third season in Houston, I thought it was time. We had lost to the New York Red Bulls in the quarter-finals of the 2008 MLS Cup Playoffs. Our dream of a three-peat was over. New York had a good team that year. Juan Pablo Angel was still at the top of his game. They went on to lose in the final two weeks later. I really thought we could have reached the MLS Cup Final again. The fact that we didn't felt like a sign from above. I couldn't leave if we had won another championship.

I had been thinking about a move for months. Everything in Houston was great, and it may sound strange, but I didn't like how comfortable I had become. I'm a firm believer that your comfort zone will kill you. My mind was telling me I needed a new challenge, and my heart was looking in only one direction.

I saw what Toronto was building and I wanted to be there to take things to the next level. I had won four titles, I was one of the faces of the league, and I wanted to come home to bring my city a championship.

I hadn't lived at home since 1997. The city had changed as much as I had. I wanted to know what it was like to live in Toronto as a pro, as a father. It wasn't easy, but I believed in my heart that it was time to leave the only MLS franchise I had ever known.

I pulled Dominic Kinnear aside at the Dynamo training ground. I was acting strange, and he knew what was coming. He cut me off before I could even start and said, "Look DeRo, do you want to go?"

I was nervous. This was the coach I always wanted. Straightforward, honest. We had so many incredible experiences. There's no other coach I had that relationship with. He talked to me like a person first and a player second. He cared about my mental health as much as, if not more than, my physical health. I felt like I owed the guy so much, so it was hard to tell him I wanted to make a move. But he let me go. He gave me that freedom, even though it wasn't what he wanted to do. I respect him a lot for that. He had no business letting me go; it was a benefit to me, not to him and definitely not our team.

"I know I'm gonna get in a lot of shit for this," he said as we hugged each other.

My teammates understood. They were sad to see me leave because it really felt like the end of a great period for all of us. We had been so successful together. But like Kawhi Leonard leaving the Raptors after their championship, my teammates knew how important it was for me to play at home. Making the trade happen though, was trickier than I thought it would be.

With Dom's blessing, I left it in the hands of my agent to sort it out with Toronto FC. Mo Johnston was TFC's director of soccer. Everything went through "Trader Mo." He quickly built a reputation for pulling off deals. The two of them were pretty much negotiating back and forth for some time to reach a common ground that worked for Toronto, Houston, and me. The media and the press were trying to get the scoop out of me for days.

"Yo, what's going on? It's happening? It's not happening? What's the hold up?"

The longer it dragged on, the more it bothered me, and I saw how it affected my parents and family. Everyone wanted the scoop. My brothers were getting calls; my mom was getting calls. They didn't know anything, but everyone pressed them like they were in on the negotiations. It was a really stressful time for them. I told them, "Listen, don't say anything. Just ignore all the phone calls. This is where I want to be. This is going to work out."

Toronto FC and Houston agreed to trade me for defender Julius James, plus allocation money. I was coming home.

I had dreamt about it for so long, and now I had manifested it. For the first time since I was 17, I would get to live in my hometown as a professional athlete. My parents and brothers would get to watch my kids grow up. I would play week in and week out for my community, in front of my community. It was an incredible dream come true.

Press conferences were never a big deal to me. The media had a job to do; we had a duty to represent the league and ourselves in a positive way. There wasn't much to it. My introductory press conference in Toronto was totally different.

I wanted to wear a suit that exemplified my feelings and showed my emotion. In San Jose I had an amazing bespoke suit guy, so he was one of my first phone calls.

"Listen, you've made some great pieces for me in the past. I'm about to go back to my hometown. I've been dreaming about signing there for a long time. It's a really big day for me and my family. Now I need a suit that exemplifies how happy I am to be home."

When I walked into his shop, I knew he had something special for me. He was walking around with the same confidence that I walked around with. On the phone he said he had the perfect suit, but that was all he told me. He laid down the material on a table the way an explorer would've laid down a new map to his kingdom. It was the shiniest suit I'd ever seen. The colour was like gunmetal chrome.

"Phew . . . you think that'll be too much?" I asked him.

"Naw, man. You said you wanted a boss man suit to show everybody the boss is home. This is a boss man suit."

It was incredible. I looked like $10 million when I tried it on. But I was hesitant — flashy clothes weren't really my thing. I was always very humble when talking about my success as a player. There was nothing humble about that suit. I took it home to model it for my wife. She could tell I was worried it was too much.

"Are you kidding me? This is you! You're a four-time champion! This is a champion's suit right here. This represents you. These people watching you got to know that they've got a champion coming to their city!" she said.

I wanted to make the most of that moment. Back then, it was a big deal when guys signed a new contract, and they dressed the part. They always had a nice suit and looked super clean. Now guys make the announcement on their Instagram stories, and they're just rocking whatever promo swag their agent landed them. The pageantry isn't there anymore.

I wanted people in my old neighbourhood, and all those like it, to think, "Here's one of our own who achieved greatness." I wanted every kid in Scarborough to see me on TV in that fancy suit and not only see a champion soccer player, but one of their own. Here's a local guy coming back home to win. Here's one of us coming home to win *for* us. I wanted everybody to know. In 2009, soccer still wasn't very popular. The sport wasn't getting the front-page press and the media attention like all the other sports. I didn't want them to downplay my homecoming. I wanted them to celebrate the fact that a local boy was coming back home to *win*.

A few hours before the press conference, I met head coach, John Carver, for the first time. I was really curious about him. Watching from afar, it was easy to see he wasn't like most coaches in MLS at the time. He was English, a proper Geordie. A real player's coach with a lot of Dom Kinnear qualities. The league was still pretty new to him, and he was still getting used to all the little things that make English and American pro soccer so different. He seemed very excited to work with me and had a plan right away to build a system around me — it was exciting to hear. That day was all about the hype and the show, but it was the game that brought me home.

Jimmy Brennan was the captain and had been there from day one, same with Carl Robinson and Danny Dichio. Amado Guevara had been a star with the New York Red Bulls and was showing that top quality in Toronto. Mo traded for Adrian Serioux before the season kicked off. We had a really good mix in the room, including guys I was already friends with and guys that had the experience of playing at high levels abroad. Expectations were high for that first season. They say the grass isn't always greener on the other side. The AstroTurf sure as hell is.

I expected there to be some growing pains. The organization was still very new to the league and was carving out its own path. When I came in as a visiting player, I didn't get mad about playing the game on turf in Toronto. The weather can be a real problem early in the season.

When I got there, the team was still training on turf. We would go to Cherry Beach, in Toronto, and train on turf fields owned by the city. We'd go to Oakville, a suburb outside of Toronto, and train on turf fields owned by the city. It was like I left Houston to go back in time. The club didn't have a problem with us training all over the place, wherever they could get the best deal. It was unprofessional. And I made that vocal early on. I must have driven everybody crazy. The coaching staff, Mo, the kit man, the bus drivers. Everybody. It took some time — and Real Madrid demanding they put grass down before bringing Cristiano Ronaldo and company over for a friendly — but BMO Field has a grass pitch now, and one of the best in the league. It's wild there was a time when it wasn't.

It was like a thousand things were more important to the people calling the shots back then. BMO Field wasn't even *our* field. We were sharing it with people walking their dogs or doing yoga or playing rec league ultimate Frisbee and shit. Where else in the world do you see this?

One day, Julian de Guzman and I called the city of Toronto, asking to rent the field for the whole year. We were just taking the piss with that phone call, but it blew our minds that we couldn't use the field some days because the city's contract with the team stated the field was to be used as a public space for so many days of the year. This was a professional organization, but TFC management didn't grasp that.

That all changed when Tim Leiweke showed up. I wonder what his first few days must've been like as President and CEO of MLSE. I picture him at the end of this long 50-person table, saying, "Look, you guys better wake the fuck up because this sport is here to take over. It's coming fast. And it's coming hard." When Tim showed up, fans weren't filling the stadium every matchday anymore. Tickets weren't hot. Once they started winning, though, it changed. Thirty thousand plus in attendance, sold out every game. People wearing TFC jerseys all around the city, game day or not. Record TV ratings. Tim was in charge for less than two years, but he changed TFC in countless ways, and also left a legacy with the Leafs and Raptors that will last a lifetime.

I look back at my first season in Toronto and see that the turf problem was a blessing in disguise. It forced me to find my loud voice. It made me the most vocal guy on the team. When it came to my city and the future of the sport in my city and my country, I wouldn't accept anything less than first class.

I started the season by telling my teammates, "Look, I'm playing to be MVP this year. And every man in this room should be playing to be MVP this year. Every defender should be playing to be Defender of the Year. Goalkeeper should be playing to be Goalkeeper of the Year. We should all be fighting to be on the MLS Best XI team at the end of the year." That's what it takes to be successful. Once you make one All-Star Game, you want another. The All-Star environment is a success building environment. TFC was missing that ingredient: the hunger for success.

We started that 2009 season on the road with a win in Kansas City. We had some pretty good results during pre-season, so to start the regular season against opposition at your level and win on the road was a good feeling for the group. We drew our next game in Columbus and then came back for my first game in Toronto as a TFC player. Homecoming for the hometown kid. I had been dreaming about that game forever. When it finally came, it was like I had been dreaming about something else.

Our home opener was against the Seattle Sounders. This was their first season in MLS. Usually expansion teams hit some bumps in the road early on, but they were a professional set-up before they made the jump to MLS. They signed Swedish star Freddie Ljungberg to show the soccer world they were big time now. He scored 15 minutes into the game, his first MLS goal. It sucked the life out of our team. It was like everyone was terrified he would score a hat trick and embarrass us. I wanted to score a hat trick that day! Maybe I wanted the game too much — nothing seemed to really go my way that afternoon. Seattle beat us 2–0. I remember sitting at my locker, just staring at the floor. I made the media wait a lot longer to speak to me than I usually did. I wanted to shake the feeling of how shit that felt before I got up and said anything. I also knew right there, I never wanted to feel that way again.

Getting used to a new environment always has its challenges. I knew right away I wasn't in Houston or San Jose. But I saw enough signs, and we definitely had enough guys in the room who made me think we could get close to that level on the field. John Carver had a much harder time getting used to things. MLS officials drove him crazy. He kept getting fined for calling out the referees and criticizing the officials every time he didn't like something. I think John was paranoid that we were getting more calls against us because of him.

Six games into the season, John resigned. I was really disappointed. I liked what he was doing before I joined the team, and after a strong pre-season, I thought we would get through the bumps we were experiencing. He didn't think so. A week before he stepped down, he told me it would be the best move for everybody. I told him I didn't agree, but that I respected his choice and valued our time together.

As bad as things were, I believed TFC could qualify for the MLS Cup Playoffs. I wasn't expecting to reach the MLS Cup Final, but we had the team to take Toronto to the playoffs for the first time. There was a trophy we had every reason to win though, the Nutrilite Canadian Championship. When the schedule came out, I told myself, "We are winning this. I don't give a shit what I've got to do, we are winning. I'm gonna make us win."

The Vancouver Whitecaps and Montreal Impact weren't MLS clubs back then. Each club played a home and away match against each other. The team with the most points after four matches would be crowned the champions and awarded a berth in the CONCACAF Champions League.

To this day, no MLS team has won the Champions League. My last year in Houston, I thought we were going to be the ones. Everything had come together for us. After winning back-to-back MLS Cups, the Dynamo got a great draw and the powerhouse Mexican clubs were knocked out. It was nearly an all MLS final. D.C. United were running through the other side of the bracket. We beat Guatemalan club Municipal in the quarter-finals. They held us to a 0–0 draw down there. I scored a brace in the return leg in Houston, and we went through 3–1 on aggregate. That should have set up a semifinal against Liga MX side Atlante, but they were upset by Deportivo Saprissa in the quarters. So it was just the Costa Ricans standing in our way of the final. But we dropped the ball at home. We couldn't score and headed south after a 0–0 draw. Their fans were so ready for us. There was an angry mob at the airport waiting for us, which is normal for that part of the world, but serious for this competition. They were thinking the same way we were: "It's just an MLS club standing in our way of the final!" There were fireworks going off outside the hotel before we checked in, and I'm pretty sure they were still going at breakfast. The vibe in the stadium was crazy. It felt like a final. Twenty-three thousand people wishing their team would wipe the turf with us. And they did. We were prepared for war that night, but everything got to us. The fans were raging before we got to the stadium for warm-ups. We were playing on turf. They scored first. The Mexican referee wasn't doing us any favours either. We lost 3–0, and that was it. Dream dead.

I wanted TFC to have that Champions League experience. I wanted fans in Toronto to see some of the best teams in the region, and I wanted my teammates to feel what it was like to go up against Mexican and Central American teams. Better opposition only makes you better. That year in the Canadian Championship, we were so much better than

Age 9, competing for Ocean Club Taekwondo.

Coolest kid on the block in my MJ & Spike Lee T-shirt, age 11.

Dad would take us down to the Scarborough Bluffs all the time.

Aunt Lea was an angel to my brothers and me.

Didn't matter how old Paul, Mark, and I got, Aunt Lea always looked after us.

Long before the braids, I was known for my curls.

Hanging out with my brothers.

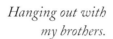

Diaper days with my bros, Paul and Mark.

DWAYNE DE ROSARIO

ABOVE: *A vintage photo of my family when I was a baby, gathered on the couch before heading out in the snow.*

RIGHT: *My family.*

DWAYNE DE ROSARIO

DWAYNE DE ROSARIO

LEFT: *You're never too young to dress for the job you want.*

Mark and I, with Adriel and Dominic from the legendary Scarborough hip-hop group Brass Tacks, November 1999.

The early days of love in Virginia. I met my wife, Brandy, while playing for the Richmond Kickers.

There's no place like Disneyland. Family vacations always go by too fast.

Loved bringing my all-stars out on gala nights. Houston Dynamo gala, 2008.

My dad didn't wear a suit and tie very often, but he always looked super fresh when he did. Toronto area gala, 2009.

Dad "Coach Tony D" and Uncle Stan Woolford coached our Malvern Magic to a Robbie Tournament win at Birchmount Stadium, and numerous other cups.

Couldn't stop Boys in Blue when we got on the pitch. Iman United, named after my nickname, won the Scarborough Indoor Soccer League.

The Earthquakes worked with the local police department to create a safe soccer program for young kids from underserved neighbourhoods. (Most were already in gangs.)

Canadian National Team picture, at the 1997 FIFA World Youth Championship in Malaysia.

Meant a lot to me to captain my hometown team in the CONCACAF Champions League.

ABOVE: *My final season at D.C. United didn't go the way I had hoped, 2013.*

Hoisting the Voyageurs Cup after the Miracle in Montreal. What a feeling!

Really wanted to take Canada to South Africa for the 2010 World Cup.

I had a lot to celebrate during my years in Houston.

I was never afraid to mix it up, especially in the CONCACAF Champions League, where we always had to prove ourselves against Mexico's best.

One of my greatest inspirations, "The Phenomenon" Ronaldo, coached my team at a Legends game in Armenia before the 2018 World Cup in Russia.

First MLS Cup in Columbus in 2001. Nobody was going to stop me.

The trials at FC Barcelona, 1996.

RICHMOND **KICKERS** PRO SOCCER

Richmond Camera

10   20

1999 #14 Dwayne DeRosario-fm
Member of the U-23 Canadian National Team.

LEFT: *Making my mark as a pro with the Richmond Kickers, 1999.*

BELOW: *San Jose Earthquakes training session, 2001.*

One of the few team picture days when I didn't have to get my hair done.

Came just short of playing at the 2000 Olympics in Sydney. USA and Honduras won the two CONCACAF spots in qualifying.

Team Canada, the 2000 CONCACAF Gold Cup champions and the only team other than USA or Mexico to ever lift that trophy.

ABOVE: *When Jason (Bent) and I weren't on the pitch, we were watching and learning.*

RIGHT: *I was named MLS Cup MVP after scoring the golden goal to win the 2001 MLS Cup, in my first season for San Jose Earthquakes.*

Battling Belize in Kingston, Ontario, in a 2006 FIFA World Cup qualifier.

MIGUEL RIOPA

I was never in awe of any player. But it's pretty cool to tell my kids I played against Cristiano Ronaldo.

CANADA SOCCER. AP VIENNA

Big strides for big strikes. My signature.

LEFT: *Back-to-back MLS Cup champions, 2007. RFK Stadium.*

BELOW: *I loved the test of going up against big clubs like Chelsea and big players like Frank Lampard, 2006 MLS All-Star Game. Toyota Park.*

David Beckham wanted a real Toronto experience and came out to my Toronto All-Star Game party.

Christmas 2019. Our last family picture with Mom and Dad. Days like this will never be the same.

Titles are always sweeter when you win at home. Celebrating TFC's second Canadian Championship with my kids, Asha, Osaze, and Adisa; and my nieces, Paul's daughters, Alyssa and Malia.

As defending Canadian champions, we were determined to keep the trophy in Toronto.

Every international match against Panama was a battle, 2011 CONCACAF Gold Cup. Livestrong Sporting Park, Kansas City, MO.

My trademark shake 'n bake goal celebration — a nod to all the man dem in Scarborough and community-housing kids I played with growing up, 2011 CONCACAF Gold Cup. Livestrong Sporting Park, Kansas City, MO.

Loved when the fans in my hometown turned out to support the national team. 2014 World Cup qualifier vs. Panama, 2012. BMO Field.

ABOVE: *Qualifying for the World Cup is the only thing Atiba (Hutchinson) and I had on our minds when we pulled on that red shirt.*

LEFT: *Blessed to have played with Julian (de Guzman) for club and country.*

The injury in Panama that changed my life.

Dressed in blue, celebrating Canada Soccer's centennial anniversary, June 3, 2012. BMO Field.

RIGHT: *The spotlight was always on Landon Donovan and me.*

BELOW: *Teammates in San Jose. Forever rivals in international soccer, Centennial match 2012. BMO Field.*

I was hungry to win again as soon as I got to New York, 2011. Red Bull Arena.

As part of Jermain Defoe's move to TFC, Tim Leiweke made sure Tottenham came over for a game. There's no such thing as a friendly match to me, 2014. BMO Field.

My return to Toronto FC sadly didn't go the way I had hoped on the pitch, 2014. BMO Field.

Loved playing in front of my hometown fans. One of the highlights of my career.

I was dialed in on matchday from the second I woke up until the final whistle, 2014 World Cup qualifier vs. Panama, 2012. BMO Field.

I guess the scouting report to Kyle Beckerman was, "The only way to stop DeRo is to grab hold of him!" 2013 friendly. Houston, TX.

ABOVE: *Honoured by Canada Soccer for my 20 years in the Canadian National Team program.*

LEFT: *Catching a Toronto Raptors game with my dad.*

RIGHT: *Drake put the 6ix on the map. Great to see a Toronto man at the top of the music game.*

BELOW: *Tinashe took over the show at my retirement press conference.*

DWAYNE DE ROSARIO

AMIL DELIC

Reunited with the two MLS Cups I won in Houston, 2017.

Helping Serena Williams build Salt Marsh Primary school in Jamaica, 2015.

On the field with some kids from my DeRo Foundation. After school programs and safe spaces are so important for kids from underserved communities, like the one I grew up in.

Loved when we could get all the De Rosario boys together and catch a Raptors game.

ABOVE: *One of the last pictures I have with my father, presenting him with the Community Excellence award at my 2020 DeRo Foundation Gala.*

ABOVE: *Three generations of football lovers.*

LEFT: *Championships bring all the stars out. NBA Finals, 2019. From left to right: Patrice Evra, Sebastian Giovinco, me, and Thierry Henry.*

Vancouver and Montreal. They were dreaming of playing in MLS. We were already doing it.

After winning our first two games at home, we lost in Vancouver and put ourselves in a hole. We played a really shitty game, and we knew we needed to win our next game in Montreal by at least four goals, or the Whitecaps would be Canadian champions. I was so pissed when we walked back into our locker room. I wanted to fight my whole team. It wasn't the performance on the field that had me fuming, it was our attitude. In the locker room, it was quiet; nobody said anything. I knew the guys were mad, but it definitely didn't feel like they were as angry as I was. There was this acceptance, like they thought, "Oh well, there's always next year." The hunger wasn't there. That's what pissed me off the most.

You can do really stupid things when you're angry. I ran up to the giant Gatorade jug in the middle of the room and kicked it as hard as I could. I thought I had sliced my toe in half. The pain rushed through my right foot, like my toes were on fire. I played it off like I was fine and hobbled back to my locker in a dancing rage. I sat down and yelled some more just to take my mind off the pain. Fighting everyone didn't seem so important anymore. I really thought I had damaged my toe so bad I might not be able to play. Wouldn't that have been some karma?

I walked around pretty uncomfortable for a few days. Thankfully my toe was just bruised and I didn't have to miss any game time. And somehow, I didn't get fined. That was a nice win in itself. But I had to wrap my head around how we were going to win our next game by four goals. No matter your opposition, winning by that big of a margin is a very difficult thing to do on the road.

On matchdays I'd spend the whole day sleeping and visualizing the game. On the bus ride to the stadium, I don't think I said a word to anyone but the bus driver on the way out. I was hyper-focused, and maybe the team fed off that. The hunger and desire was there in the whole team. We knew the odds were against us, but we were ready to do something special for the big group of fans who made the drive up Highway 401, and for our new manager, Chris Cummings. And then

Montreal scored from a penalty kick, 20 minutes into the game. Now we needed five goals!

This rush of anger came over me, just like when I kicked the jug in the dressing room. How could we let that happen, knowing the pressure we were under? We just handed them the chance to bury us. It felt like a punch in the face. Nick Garcia had tackled their forward from behind. It was a lazy play that was easy for the referee to spot. Nick was an experienced guy and there was no threat. That's what really frustrated me. But as much as I wanted to run over and cuss him out, I knew no good would come from it. When you're a leader on the team, you have to master the fine balance of being angry with mistakes and recognizing that that player knows they messed up and motivating them to put it behind them. I looked at Nick and said, "There's lots of game left. Let's make up for that!" I think Nick went on to play one of the best games he played all year.

After giving up that opening goal, I knew we needed something spectacular to grow the fire. I made a run up the wing and had all this space in front of me. I could see Danny Dichio running down the centre of the field, so I curled this perfect ball into the box. He dove for it and stretched his neck out as far as he could but couldn't head it into the net. He looked up at me with such disappointment. He wanted to put that in as much as I wanted him to. But it was a start. We were either gonna go out guns blazin', or we were gonna roll over and die. I never chose the second option. Ever.

Chris had worked on set pieces with us a lot in training. The corner kick came in and Montreal's keeper ran out to punch it away before Danny could get his head on it, but he didn't get much on it and punched it just over my head, seven yards out. With my back to the net, I leaned back all the way and bicycle kicked it into the bottom corner. I sprinted back to the centre circle, yelling, "LET'S GO!" the entire way. We had one. About 10 minutes later, Jimmy swung a ball in that sailed over everyone and fell to me at the top of the box. I looked down and smashed it. It took a deflection off the defender but hit the bottom corner of the net. Now we had two, and we had made Montreal nervous. I wonder what the team talk was like in their locker room at halftime? Probably something along the lines of, "Whatever you do, just stop De Rosario!"

It was going to take a lot more than 11 guys that night, though. I wanted that championship. And I wanted a hat trick. There was a real energy in the room when we walked in at halftime. Chris was talking tactics and what he wanted to see in the second half when I got up and cut him off. I looked every player in the eye and said, "Listen! This is straightforward now, guys. It's either we go out and roll over and let those fans down. Or we go out there with those fans behind us and give it everything we got!"

We stormed out of the room with the mentality that we could succeed. Every guy found just a little more energy. We didn't let Montreal breathe. They started playing with a really high line, trying to get us with the offside trap. I made a great run past my defender and got the perfect ball. I took three touches and smashed it low again. Now I had three, and we had a real chance. Our travelling fans went crazy. It sounded like there were three times as many TFC fans in that stadium. That really motivated our whole team.

With 20 minutes to go, we got a free kick at the top of the box on the left side. I wanted to smash it over the wall of players and pick out the top corner. I stood over the ball with Amado Guevara and I could tell he had the same idea. He had this look in his eye. He didn't even have to say anything. He ran up and blasted the ball into the back of the net. It was the type of free kick goal that Sebastian Giovinco would score often for TFC a few years later. Amado was great at those, and no keeper could have stopped that shot that night. We rushed back to the centre circle, buzzing. Four down, one more to go.

Montreal took forever to restart the game. This confusion had swept over every player in white, like a fog. They all looked lost. Their heads went down farther and farther after every goal we scored. I was feeding off that. We set up for a corner kick, and they didn't know what to do. Amado went over to take it, and I knew if it landed in the box, one of us would put it in. Montreal were totally scrambled, no one could keep hold of their man. Chad Barrett got free and headed it in. Goal number five.

The football gods were looking down on us that day. It was the first time Toronto FC had ever scored five goals in a match. Amado added one more to put the cherry on top and to really suck the life out of the Vancouver Whitecaps, who were watching from above. They had flown out from Vancouver, expecting to be on the field celebrating their championship. When the referee blew the final whistle, this red wave of emotion swept over the whole stadium. Our bench stormed the field, and everyone was hugging and jumping all over each other. We knew we were capable of it, but the feeling that washes over you at the very moment you accomplish your goal is indescribable. I ran straight over to celebrate with our fans. They cheered us on the entire time and never gave up. It meant so much to me to share that moment with them. It was historic. It was the "Miracle in Montreal."

I don't think people really understand what we did that day. Comebacks like that are almost unheard of in soccer. We were the first group of Toronto FC players to raise a trophy over our heads. It was the first championship for MLSE in 42 years. We celebrated like we had won MLS Cup. It's a feeling I will never forget. I came to Toronto to win trophies, and we did with our first chance. I really thought it would be the first of many.

CHAPTER 10

THE BEGINNING OF THE END

I am allergic to losing. It literally causes me physical trauma. My head hurts. My stomach hurts. If I was left alone to think about the failure, I would actually vomit.

If my team was losing, I could not be happy. My kids would tell my wife, "Dad lost. We know that we can't talk to him. He's a bad one." When I think about that now, it breaks my heart a little. But back then, it was the damn truth.

I really took losing games personally. Why couldn't I make my team win? What was I doing wrong out there? What didn't I do to prepare my team to win?

I didn't have many of those bad days in San Jose and Houston. Winning is in my DNA. Yeah, the money was good and it was good to be home, but football was my life.

In Toronto, I didn't smell championships. I couldn't taste success. Those feelings that were so much a part of my career in San Jose and Houston didn't exist in Toronto. As hard as I tried to recreate them, they couldn't exist with the climate of instability and inexperience that engulfed the club.

My first season was unlike any other. We missed the playoffs by getting our asses played off the pitch in New York in the last game of the season. It was embarrassing. The rain was horrendous that day. I felt like the soccer gods were torturing me.

We had three coaching changes in one year. That doesn't happen anywhere, in any sport. Everywhere I had been before, there was consistency, and we had success because of it. That didn't exist in Toronto. It was frustrating.

I did my best to block out the distractions and just focus on my game and keeping my teammates motivated. We had to do what we could do as players: focus on the field and not let that stuff affect us. But it wasn't easy, especially for the younger guys.

I became the Dr. Phil of the dressing room. Everyone came to me for advice and to share their thoughts and fears. They were my brothers, and I always had their backs. But I couldn't believe there was little to no support from the club. It was as if no one recognized how the revolving door of coaches and players was affecting the product we put out on the field.

Being a leader has its challenges. I had been overcoming challenges my entire life. In my career, I always found a way to win in the end. But in Toronto, winning felt impossible. And because of that, winning became secondary.

Season two was supposed to be a fresh start. Mo hired his old teammate Preki to be the club's fourth head coach in four seasons. They had played on the Kansas City Wizards together for years. Preki had a reputation for being a real hard ass on the pitch. He always got stuck in hard on tackles and played with a real chip on his shoulder. The kind of guy you'd want on your team but you'd hate to play against. At least, that's what it seemed like when I was playing against him at the end of his career.

Preki had played with Red Star Belgrade, known as one of the toughest clubs in the world, in the 1980s. He came over to the United States and was an indoor soccer star for years before playing for Everton and then finishing his career in MLS. He went straight into coaching when he retired and was Bob Bradley's assistant coach at Chivas USA. When Bob got the U.S. Men's National Team job, Chivas promoted

Preki to head coach. There was a lot of hype around him. He was one of the few guys who had played in the league as it had grown and developed and now was coaching the next crop. There were probably a few MLS clubs after him when his pal Mo came calling. I really hoped Preki's presence would be the spark we needed. Right away I could see that he had it out for me.

Preki always wanted to challenge me. We'd start a training session, and he'd come over and want to compete with me in a crossbar challenge or keep-ups.

"DeRo! A hundred dollars I hit the crossbar with my first shot!"

"Five hundred dollars I keep the ball up longer than you!"

"What are you, scared? Let's do this!"

It was weird, man. He'd challenge me to play basketball against him, cards, literally anything. At first I thought it was just his way of getting involved with the group, and he was singling me out because I was the captain, so that was his in. But then it felt like he was just obsessed with competing against me. He took everything so seriously and never wanted to be outdone. I'd been around a lot of guys with big egos, but his was something else.

Every time Brandy and I moved to a new place, we stayed away from the hustle and bustle of the city. I was all about my career, and the suburbs just seemed like a much better fit for us and the kids. When I got traded to Toronto, I knew that the closer I was to Scarborough, the more distractions I'd have. We bought a house in Oakville. The two communities couldn't be more different. Literally opposites on the map, and in lifestyle. I wanted to stay focused on my game. Toronto FC's world-class training ground wasn't built yet, and we held all our training sessions in Oakville. It was the perfect scenario for me. Anyone who has ever driven in Toronto knows the traffic is the worst. Most of the players lived in condos downtown. They would show up at BMO Field every morning and take the team bus out to Oakville. Preki demanded I drive into Toronto to join the team on the bus ride out to Oakville. It was a 45-kilometre drive. That seemed crazier to me than sharing the field with the city and then renting it out for yoga classes and kids sports.

I said to him, "Coach, I live a few minutes from the training ground. Why would I drive for an hour in rush hour to take the bus back there, and then take the bus back downtown only to drive home again in traffic?"

Preki looked at me very seriously and crossed his hands behind his back as he spoke to me.

"You're the captain. You need to be a leader and show them you're one of them, not above them."

I didn't think I was above them. I just didn't think that made any sense. Why couldn't I just meet the bus at training? The same should've been acceptable for any player who lived in Oakville. Some guys deserved certain privileges. Didn't he get that? He was a U.S. international — I'm sure he wasn't treated like the rest of the guys when he was a player.

There was a distance with Preki that I had never experienced with a coach before. Whenever there was an issue with Dom or Frank, they would bring all the senior players together and talk about what was going on. Preki didn't do that. Days would go by and he wouldn't talk to me. One day his assistant coach, Leo Percovich, asked me why it seemed like Preki was always in competition with me. "You should ask him," I said.

The hotter the weather got, the worse things got for the team. Preki had assembled a team of workers, not footballers. It was like he was running a crossfit gym instead of a soccer team. I must admit he got me to a fitness level that I had never been at before because all we did was run. In his mind, we weren't as technical as the other teams, so we had to outwork everybody to get anything. But hard work only gets you so far in the pros. Preki wanted guys to bust their asses until they threw up. We would get off the plane and go straight to training. That wasn't normal. During the World Cup break, he had us training the entire time. He was running guys into the ground and didn't see the negative effect it was having. To him, if his players didn't like it, "Well, too bad — they're not good enough to not have to work this hard." That's when guys really quit on him.

Losing always makes everything worse. Preki played around with different things and tried to make a lot of changes, but so many guys felt left out because of how he had treated them during the year that by that point, they didn't want to put the work in for him. We didn't have the talent and the quality to play the systems he was trying to play. I was doing more than my job. I was playing midfield, I was playing forward. I was running more miles than I ever had, with little to no results.

At halftime of a Champions League match in Panama, I lost it in the dressing room. We were playing C.D. Árabe Unido at this small, shitty stadium. It was hot, the facilities were bad, there was a giant running track around the field that Preki was going to make us run around at the end of the game. I couldn't take it anymore, and I snapped on him. I don't remember what I said, I was just so frustrated. But that was the moment I felt like the season was lost.

In my experience, it didn't matter what formations and tricks you tried if you didn't have your players out there wanting to play and win for you. Managing individuals and getting everyone on board was the recipe for success. Not everybody had to like each other, but everyone had to buy in. At the end of the day, everybody has to respect the manager and play for him. When you look across the board, most of the successful teams are managed by men that players like. Mourinho lost his way at some point — maybe he got too big for himself — but he was applauded for how well he managed players. Same with Pep Guardiola, Jürgen Klopp, and Diego Simeone. Players will go through a wall for guys like that. Dom and Frank were like that. Dom never made a player feel bad in public: he always took the blame. Dom blamed himself in front of the media all the time to protect us in Houston. That's managing. There were stretches where we had a bad losing streak, and a division would build between the defenders and midfielders or the keeper and his defenders. A good manager knows how important it is to nip that right in the bud.

There was so much bullshit going on in my second season in Toronto. There was this disconnect from the management to the coaches, from the coaches to the players. Everything seemed disorganized and very little made sense.

It's no secret that there's a lot of sweet-talking that goes on in professional sports negotiations. But in my experience, honesty and hard work were valued and rewarded. That changed when I came to Toronto.

In a salary cap system, it's very difficult for players to be paid what they're worth. Even now that salaries have gone up, there are countless underpaid players. MLS clubs have clever ways to reward a guy without impacting the team's cap dramatically. It's so complicated, even the media doesn't understand all the money tricks involved. And the rules change all the time.

When I came to Toronto, I wasn't about the gimmicks. I didn't want cars and condos like some guys. After the success I had in the league, I wanted to be a designated player — a league designation created when David Beckham joined the LA Galaxy, which allows a team to pay up to three players any salary, with only a percentage counting against the team's salary cap.

I wanted to be the first Canadian DP in MLS history. Mo Johnston agreed I should be. My trade from Houston was initiated under that condition and was really what got the ball rolling. But once my trade was finalized, "DP" wasn't in my contract.

Interesting tactic to use on somebody with an unrivalled resume in a league you are still new to . . . Mo assured me that it was not his fault. He blamed the bureaucracy of a corporate boardroom ownership group. Every team in the league has three DP spots available, but there's no obligation to use them. Toronto FC believed they could put a winning team on the field without exhausting their resources and paying more for better players. Like me, Mo knew that was impossible. He assured me I would get a DP contract at the end of my first season.

I don't know what's worse: that he was able to tell me that with a straight face or that I believed him. I had signed the contract in good faith that a great season would be rewarded with a new deal and a designated player contract. That didn't happen.

At the end of my first season, TFC signed Julian de Guzman to the first designated player deal in franchise history. I was thrilled for my friend. He was an incredible player and starred in Spain's top division for four years. JDG was the first Canadian ever to play in La Liga. That was historic.

Julian is like my little brother. He is three years younger than me, but the soccer circle in Scarborough is a small and tight one. His family and mine knew each other from the early days. Because of the age difference, the game took us down different roads. But Julian and I always stayed close. We almost started our careers in Europe together.

François Glasman was a Canadian coach who had a lot of contacts within France and would take a bunch of Canadian kids over on trials. There's a long list of players he celebrates having "discovered" and introduced to clubs throughout France and the rest of Europe. François took Julian and me on trial to Olympique de Marseille together. They were the biggest team in France at the time, and one of the biggest in the world in the 1990s. Marseille won the Champions League in 1993 and was known to have a lot of money — how much of it was legal is a story for another day. But it was well known that soccer money flowed in the south of France.

François totally fucked me. Marseille was interested and thought they could work me into the first team after some time with the reserves. He told the club the price for Julian and me was $4 million. We were a combo deal, take it or leave it. Marseille said no. That was crazy money for unproven kids from Canada. And that was the end of it for me. Julian ended up in Marseille's development academy, and that was the start of his professional career in Europe. A few years later, his brother Jonathan followed in his footsteps and went over, even younger, to Holland. We know how well that worked out for Jono.

Signing Julian in 2009 was a massive move for TFC as a club and for our squad that was dying for quality. It was a big moment for the league to get a guy in his prime that was performing in Europe to come over. And Toronto was the only club he was going to leave Spain for. It was a dream come true for Jules.

But I felt betrayed. That was supposed to be my deal — I came home to get that. I was promised I would get that, but all I heard was excuse after excuse. The club blamed the league; the league made clear that DP contracts were decided by the clubs. It was important for me to be a designated player because everybody else was getting it. Landon Donovan had been rewarded for being a superstar in the league. I was getting paid well, so why couldn't I have that same status? Because I hadn't made my name in Europe? Because I'm Canadian? That's how it felt.

Selfishly, yes, I wanted the status of being a DP. And the money was a good perk. But I also wanted the league to step out of this box, to show everyone that MLS wasn't just a place where good players come to retire and get paid. If you perform here, you should get rewarded here. What example does it set for kids growing up here who want to be pros? They have to leave their families and head overseas so they can have a chance to play and get paid? That's not right. And neither were the way things were going in Toronto.

It was clear that Preki's team needed more quality. Scoring goals always comes at a premium. During the 2010 World Cup, while we were grinding our asses training, TFC signed Julian's former Deportivo de La Coruña teammate, Mista, to a $1 million DP contract.

Fool me once, shame on you. Fool me twice, shame on me, right?

From that moment, things were never the same. I became a different person, one who couldn't dismiss the feeling that I wasn't being appreciated for all my hard work and dedication. No player took the losses to heart the way I did. I was letting down my city every time my team couldn't deliver. I was scoring goals and doing my best to give us a chance to win. But the club felt a Spanish guy who probably had never even watched an MLS game before was more deserving of that money than me?

Mo Johnston owed me and he knew it. He would avoid me at the training ground and the stadium but then praise me every time he was in front of the media.

"DeRo is the heart and soul of this team . . ."

"He's the best player this club has ever had . . ."

"We wouldn't even have been in that match if it wasn't for Dwayne."

At the end of the season, I was gonna get mine and then some. I was making a fraction of what JDG and Mista were getting paid, but I was the team's leading goal scorer. I never stopped performing on the pitch, no matter what nonsense was going on off of it. They had to see that this time.

Midway through September, Mo Johnston and Preki were fired.

Fuck!

Preki had lost the room a long time before that, and we were never going to make the playoffs. But I was more concerned with the new management group that would come in and put their own stamp on the team. Promises were made to me that hadn't been kept. The last thing I wanted was a new group to deal with.

On matchdays, I could block out any noise. Whatever was bothering me no longer mattered. All I cared about was winning and leaving everything I had out there on the pitch. The only people who knew how frustrated I was about my contract were Mo, my agent, and my wife. I was professional through all the chaos on and off the pitch. That's how my dad raised me.

I scored both goals in our first match after the firings, a 2–1 win on the road against my old Dynamo. I was even more motivated to prove my worth.

The next week we were at BMO Field for our second-last home game of the season. Chris Wondolowski scored two goals to give San Jose a 2–0 lead. He's one of the most lethal goal scorers to ever play in MLS and was so good at creating something out of nothing. A goal from the away team usually sucks the energy out of a building. It was even quicker when it was Wondo on the scoresheet.

It felt like one of those games that was going to get out of hand really quickly if we didn't make something happen. Just after the hour mark, I saw my chance. I chipped a shot from the edge of the 18-yard box into the top right corner. It was a big-time goal and brought the stadium to life.

But instead of celebrating with my go-to shake 'n bake DeRo shuffle, I ran towards the cameras on the sideline and mockingly wrote myself a big fat cheque. I didn't plan it — it just happened. I had been playing with this weight on my shoulders for weeks; it was just my natural reaction to celebrate like that. And I felt great.

I had no idea that would be the beginning of the end of my marriage with TFC.

CHAPTER 11

CRAVING A BIGGER STAGE

A few weeks before the 2008 MLS All-Star Game in Toronto, I got a real All-Star experience testing my skills against some of the best players around. The Free Kick Masters competition was a travelling road show, pitting top players against top goalkeepers. Think about it like soccer's version of the NBA Slam Dunk Contest or MLB's Home Run Derby.

They set up a wall for players to hit free kicks over at real goalkeepers. Some of the very best put on the gloves, including Francesco Toldo, David James, Kasey Keller, and Jorge Campos. The kickers were pretty good too: Romário, Robert Pires, Sulley Muntari, Júlio Baptista, Javier Portillo, Segundo Castillo, and Jozy Altidore. Ronaldinho was the headliner. He was the best player in the world. And he brought this kid that was just starting to come through at Barcelona: Lionel Messi.

Ronaldinho has this swagger about him that's just badass. Everything about him is cool, and he lights up a room when he walks in. But he can flip that switch and all of a sudden, he's like, "I'm gonna mess shit up if I need to right now," on or off the field. He came over to chat with my kids and was kicking balls around with them, which was a really memorable moment for me. He bought out the top floor at the Four Seasons and threw the craziest parties. Ronaldinho had built a reputation in Spain for having a party game as good as his skills on the field. It was pretty accurate.

The winner got $1 million, and the Golden Goalkeeper won $500,000. I wanted that $1 million, and I had one big advantage over everybody else. The event was in Houston at Reliant Stadium. My teammate Brad Davis also participated, so he got some love too. But I definitely felt the love from the twenty thousand fans when I stepped up.

The format was one-v-one heads up against a goalkeeper. My first test: Mexican star, and my future teammate, Rafael Márquez. We were shooting on Francesco Toldo. I scored my first two shots, and the crowd went crazy. I put such a curve on my second ball, and it bent like one of those famous Roberto Carlos shots. It's a pretty cool feeling when you do something that has Ronaldinho picking his jaw up off the floor. Most of the guys reacted like an NBA bench does after a big dunk. I didn't get enough on the third shot, and Toldo turned it aside. Márquez stepped up and scored all three. Just like that, I was out. But what an experience. I had my moment with the best, and I gave the crowd a show. My crowd. In the end, Márquez walked away with the $1 million, so at least I can say I lost to the winner. David James was the Golden Goalkeeper.

That weekend, a few of those guys asked me why I wasn't playing in Europe. Every player has a list of "What if?" stories or "I guess it wasn't meant to be" experiences. My list felt really long. I sat down for a drink at one of Ronaldinho's hotel parties, looking at the crowd, wondering what it would be like to have played against some of those guys week in and week out. Ronaldinho came over to me with a couple of glasses and poured us a drink. He asked the same question. "You know, I know some good agents who want to be involved in American sports too. I can introduce you to them," he told me.

It's not like I hadn't tried. Every time I went to pursue that European dream, it just didn't work out in my favour. Whether it was mismanagement or not my time, it never happened. I thought it was going to in 2005.

Blackburn Rovers F.C. wanted me. Ten years removed from winning the Premier League title, they were a famous club trying to keep a strong foot in a league where they couldn't spend like the big boys. The trial came about through future Toronto FC head coach, Ryan Nelsen. We had the same agent at the time. I trained with Blackburn for two or three weeks. Mark Hughes, the manager, was playing for Blackburn just a few years before and was a highly rated up-and-coming coach. With all his success playing for Manchester United, he was bound to make a name for himself in management. Mark is a real players coach. I noticed very quickly all his players had a lot of respect for him, like he had been in charge for 10 or 15 years.

I played a 90-minute match with Blackburn's reserves against Ryan and the rest of Blackburn's first team. I scored a hat trick in that game. Going up against Premier League players was really motivating, and I impressed a lot of people that day, Ryan included. Mark Hughes had plenty of kind words for me, and I thought I'd be walking away with a contract. I left the stadium thinking I'd get home only to pack my bags and get back on a plane with my wife and kids. But MLS wanted a lot of money. I heard at least $4 million, if not $6 million. Blackburn wouldn't meet their price. Opportunity gone. Just like that.

I don't blame Blackburn for not paying that transfer fee. They weren't the kind of club that was spending that on anyone. That's when I started to get really frustrated with the league. How could they ask for that much money, when they were paying me so little in comparison? I wasn't even making 10 percent of that. Even before we found out the Earthquakes were moving to Houston, I felt like I was at a real cross-roads in my career. It seemed like Europe was the best option for me to make top dollar. I had my own marketing deal on the side and was one of the few players, to my knowledge, who had one. So I do respect MLS for removing some of the restrictions, which allowed me to earn extra income. It was nothing ludicrous, but it was something. It still wasn't European football though.

Watching Landon Donovan get a few chances in Europe, I felt like the stepchild. My agents and I had a lot of conversations about how I was performing at or near his level but was being treated like I was just a fraction of the player. Like so many North Americans playing at the time, I knew no matter what I did in MLS, the real money was overseas.

Edson Buddle was one of the best goal scorers in the league in 2010. He scored 17 to finish just one goal back of Chris Wondolowski for the MLS Golden Boot (I finished third with my 15 for TFC that season, just saying). LA Galaxy won the Supporters' Shield, thanks to Eddie's goals. He was named team MVP, and he was one of the top players in MLS. But he left one of the league's premier franchises to play for a team nobody could even pronounce in Germany's second division. Why? Because they would pay him what a World Cup experienced goal scorer deserved, or at least closer to it.

After the Blackburn trial in 2005, I was going to leave MLS when my agent worked out a deal with Russian Premier League club FC Rubin Kazan. It was a guaranteed contract, $500,000 a year. Everything came together really quickly. Before I knew it, I was sitting in the airport lounge at Toronto's Pearson International Airport, waiting for a flight. I was going to meet the team in Turkey for pre-season. "Last call for Istanbul. Last call for Istanbul." I stood up, grabbed my bag, and walked away from the gate. I didn't get on the flight.

Something came over me as I sat there and let my decision really sink in. It all had come together so fast, I hadn't had a chance to really digest what I was doing for myself and what this would do to my family. I didn't want to go there just for the money. I never wanted to be in the position where I was playing soccer for the money. It wasn't going to be easy in Russia. I would be leaving my family for two years. My kids were still young — I didn't want to sacrifice missing that. I knew I couldn't bring them over to Russia to live with me. I saw these parents at the airport with their young children, getting ready to board their flights. Some looked like they were headed off on vacation; others looked like they were dragging their kids around on a business trip. But all of those parents looked overjoyed to be with their children. Watching them in that moment, I knew I couldn't handle two years without that.

Damani Ralph went to Rubin Kazan instead. He had a couple of good seasons with the Chicago Fire and signed with Rubin for a $2 million transfer fee, or something like that. That could've been me. It wasn't, and I won two more championships in Houston because I stayed. I wouldn't trade that for double the money and two years in Russia.

———

After the cheque-signing incident in Toronto, the emotions of all the bullshit I was dealing with came to a head. I had to take that hit to come to the conclusion that I had to get out of Toronto. Every time I was banging on the walls, something happened within the management team. After the Mista signing, I made it very clear that I was going to get mine at the end of the season, then Preki and Mo got fired. A brand new executive team came in, and the conversations started from scratch.

"Well, Dwayne, you do have a contract here that you did agree to. Now, we are a brand new management team here and understand that maybe some promises were made that shouldn't have been or that were misleading. Just give us some time and we'll figure something out."

Same story, different storyteller.

I had known Earl Cochrane for a long time. He'd worked in the Canadian National Team program since I could remember and started with Toronto FC on day one. He worked his way from manager of team operations to academy director to general manager to director of team and player operations. I think Earl had only been on the job for a few days when my agent, David Baldwin, called him with a solution.

"Look, if the club can't pay Dwayne what he's asking for, let's get him a move overseas. At the very least, let's find him a loan deal with a club that would take on some of his salary, which would help you guys out and give him that chance to play in Europe. Landon Donovan and Eddie Johnson have done it — I'm sure we can find the right fit for Dwayne and everybody here."

It had become the new model. Beckham had barely planted roots in L.A. when he left for A.C. Milan for a few months. The American guys followed that lead. At the very least, I expected the same opportunity.

Scottish giants Celtic F.C. were interested in having me come out on trial. I was out with my kids in Oakville when David called to tell me.

"I've got good news and bad news, so I'll just start with the good. Celtic want you. They're willing to consider a short-term loan if that's all that they can get. The bad news is, the club is against the idea of you going over there."

The resistance didn't make sense to me. We weren't talking about some random club that was just looking to write a cheque or waste TFC's time. This was Glasgow Celtic! One of the biggest football clubs in the world. I called Earl Cochrane and asked him to meet. I forget where I was with the kids, but I wrangled them up and took them home to Brandy, so that I could make the long drive into the city. I didn't want to have the conversation in his office, and neither did he, so Earl and I met at Liberty Noodle, a Japanese restaurant close to BMO Field. I ordered the biggest pot of tea and told myself I wasn't going to look at the food menu until Earl dined on what I had to say.

"There's so much more at play here than just me playing over there, Earl. There's a lot of Scottish fans in Toronto. There's a lot of Celtic supporters that TFC could win over by developing a partnership with their club. It could expand your scouting network. It could get TFC a few pre-season friendlies. Letting me go is just a short-term thing for TFC. There's a lot of long-term gains that could come out of this."

I could see the ideas bouncing around in his head. Whatever the hesitation was when we first sat down was waning. He knew there was a much bigger picture to all this and agreed that my points made sense. Earl told me there was some paperwork that he and David had to work out, and he'd deal with whatever backlash came from ownership and the league. I got in my car and probably drove faster than I ever had down the highway.

David didn't waste any time. The winter transfer window had just opened, and Celtic were serious about improving their team to end Rangers F.C.'s back-to-back Scottish Premier League title reign. I got to spend Christmas morning at home with my family. As I watched them open all their presents, overwhelmed with joy, I couldn't wait for my big present: playing in Europe. I knew it was just a trial and I had to introduce myself to a big club that didn't know anything about me, other than a few goals they had seen on the internet. But I was confident I could win them over and finally play at a big club in Europe.

I packed my bags, and on December 27, 2010, got on a plane to Glasgow. It's one of the few dates that aren't a birthday or anniversary that I remember without hesitation. From my understanding, everything that Earl had asked for was sent, and everything was good.

I got a good night's sleep in a nice hotel, then went to Parkhead in the morning to meet Celtic's manager, Neil Lennon, and the team. I left my phone charging at the hotel. When I got back and turned it on, I thought my phone was going to explode: message after message, then voicemail notification after voicemail notification. I was starting to wonder if something foolish had happened at TFC again. Maybe they had fired the new manager before they had even hired him. Of course not. They were all about me and my off-season Scottish adventure. David was the first person I called.

"Did you see the article on MLS.com?" he asked.

"No, David. What's up?"

"TFC doesn't know why Dwayne De Rosario is training with Celtic in Scotland, without the club's permission."

He had to repeat himself because I thought, "There's no way I'm hearing him correctly." I felt like I was in a bad dream. How was that the headline on the league's website? How were there articles and news stories all over the place with the same narrative? My wife called me. My dad called me, pissed.

"The hell is wrong with you! How you go over there and not even tell these people?"

He was almost as mad with me as when I had lied to him about what happened to my eye when I was a kid.

"Dad, I sat down with the guy, gave him all the information he wanted, and he told me it was all good! David Baldwin is a big-time agent. It's not like I was gonna fly under the radar. It's Celtic! There are fans and media, taking pictures of every car and every person that rolls through the gates. I wouldn't have come here thinking TFC wouldn't know. Come on, Pops!"

Earl gave me the okay, but he hadn't cleared it with ownership. So when fans started complaining, tweeting, and raging on the radio, the club spun it around on me. Earl turned around and turtled in a corner, saying, "No, I didn't know anything about it."

But I had emails. MLS had to come in and cover for TFC because they didn't want the club to look bad. The league's stance was, "There was a misunderstanding between all three parties. Everything is okay as far as the league and our player are concerned. Dwayne is free to continue his trial at Celtic."

I spent New Year's Eve in Glasgow away from my family, alone in my hotel room. The young DeRo would've gone out and enjoyed himself. I wasn't there for that. I started training with the full squad, and Neil Lennon loved me. Georgios Samaras was Celtic's star player at the time, and he took to me straight away. We ran a lot of drills together and linked up for a ton of goals in mini games. There was an instant connection.

I wasn't the only MLS guy there looking for a deal. Celtic had brought Freddie Ljungberg over on trial with me. After a couple of successful years in Seattle, the Sounders traded him to Chicago Fire. At the end of the season, he was ready to go back to Europe. We got on really well too. We talked a lot about MLS and life as a whole. He has a very good perspective of the world, so it's no surprise he's gone into management now.

The club took us along to Ibrox in Glasgow, for the Old Firm Derby. Celtic versus Rangers is one of the biggest rivalries in all of sports. It's so much bigger than soccer; it's part of the two clubs' identities. Freddie and I rode the bus with the team to Ibrox because Neil wanted us to experience the whole atmosphere from start to finish. He wanted us to be playing in an Old Firm Derby in the near future. It is as intense as advertised. The bus was pelted with bottles and garbage. Rangers fans despise anyone and anything associated with Celtic Football Club. They weren't happy that day.

Celtic were leading Rangers by one point at the top of the standings and were determined to leave with a four-point edge. The mood on the bus ride over was very serious, and I could tell it wasn't because of the madness outside or the magnitude of the Derby. They saw this match as the one that could decide the championship that season. Samaras scored two goals, and Celtic won 2–0. It felt like a big win for me. Everyone was buzzing on the bus ride back. Neil came over and sat next to me for a minute. He was smiling from ear to ear.

"Was that something or was that something! DeRo, we want you to be here, and we're gonna push to keep you for the rest of our season."

I couldn't have been more excited to hear that. Now I was the one who was buzzing. I couldn't wait to get back so I could call my wife. We must have talked for an hour. She had a million questions I couldn't answer, but I was excited to be able to, in time. When I hung up the phone, I saw that I had 10 missed calls from my agent. I called him back, assuming he'd got a contract for me. Thrilled to have beaten their rivalries, the club didn't want to waste any time making their squad even better. Wrong.

"Dwayne, we've got a problem. TFC does not want to sell you. They're not going to let you sign with Celtic."

What the fuck? It was like I was living that same bad dream all over again.

"Hold up, David. What do you mean? They won't even consider a loan deal? They don't even have a coach! Who's saying no?"

Jürgen Klinsmann.

TFC had hired the former German star as an advisor to help the club find a new coaching staff. Klinsmann didn't want me to leave because he wanted his handpicked manager to have me as the centrepiece of the rebuild.

On Klinsmann's suggestion, Toronto FC hired Dutch coach Aron Winter. Like Klinsmann, Winter was a star player at two of the biggest clubs in the world: AFC Ajax, in Amsterdam, and Inter Milan, in Italy. Having spent a few years coaching in Ajax's famous academy, Winter was ready for a top job somewhere else. What better place to step into the fire than MLS? Paul Mariner was hired as director of player development. He was Steve Nicol's assistant in New England for years, so at least someone had some MLS experience. Both Aron and Paul made it clear that they expected every single player to be in camp from the start.

"You got to be shitting me right now," I said to David.

I told David we weren't going to take no for an answer. We didn't know how, but I wasn't getting on a plane unless I was going to get my family to bring back to Scotland. When I showed up at Celtic's training ground, Neil Lennon pulled me aside as soon as he spotted me.

"Sorry, Dwayne, you can't continue to train with the team. Celtic doesn't want any bad publicity or a bad relationship with your club and Major League Soccer. I'll be honest Dwayne, I feel really bad for you. I have never seen a situation like this in my life. I've never experienced this in my life."

There was so much truth in his eyes. I'll never forget the look on his face. To this day, I get mad just thinking about that conversation because that was "the dream is dead" moment. But I was still in denial. I called Klinsmann so that we could have a conversation without middlemen. It went a lot better than I thought it was going to.

"DeRo, don't worry. I'll take care of this. I'll talk to Aron and see that you can stay at Celtic for a few more weeks [until the start of the MLS season]. There's no reason you shouldn't be over there."

I couldn't train with Celtic, so I went to the gym a lot. I tried to distract myself by doing and seeing things around the city. I took a drive into the Highlands without a map, just to get lost. Reggae music isn't the easiest thing to find over there, but I did. I listened to it a lot; I needed that musical healing more than ever.

Winter tried calling me a bunch of times, but I didn't have anything to say to him. Klinsmann said he was going to take care of things, so that's what I was waiting for. As the days went by, I was starting to think he wouldn't. Finally I spoke with Winter on the phone. He wanted to explain why he felt it was so important I rejoined TFC for pre-season. He was not ready for my reaction.

"Pre-season? Who cares about pre-season! I've been a pro for 14 years. I don't need a fucking pre-season to be ready to play!" I yelled at him.

"Yes, I know you don't need the conditioning, but we're working some brand new systems into a brand new squad, with a lot of players who don't have the MLS experience that you do. They need their captain there. The whole squad does. You're their leader," he said to me.

"Listen, Aron. Respect to you and all you did at Inter and Holland and all that shit, but I'm a footballer too. It doesn't take much for me to adapt. And in this league that you don't know anything about, there's so much parity in the league that points don't even really matter until the summer. I can come in, and you can put me on the bench for a couple of weeks if you want to work me in and learn the system, but it's not that hard. I'll be ready. Good footballers know how to adapt. I can do that."

I thought I was being pretty reasonable. Of all the things for a new coach to obsess over, this just didn't seem like the right one, not with a guy who had proven himself in the league time and time again.

"You're our leader. I want you to lead our team. I need you to be here," he pleaded.

"Fuck, let Julian lead the team! Give him the captaincy. I don't care about the armband right now. Jules played in Spain. He's got all the experience in the world to lead this team of new players you're putting together. Let him be the captain."

"I'm not going to do that, Dwayne. The club would not want me to do that, and I do not want to do that. This is your hometown club, and I know how much that means to you. Come home and lead your team," he said and hung up the phone.

After Neil told me I couldn't continue to train with Celtic, I stayed in Scotland on my own dime for seven days. I couldn't go home. My dream of playing for a big club was right there in front of my face, and it was being snatched away. I didn't want to talk to or see anybody, not even my family. My wife called one night and we had a long talk about everything. I told her I thought maybe it was a sign I should just walk away and retire. I was 32; this was my last chance to play overseas and I was being denied. Maybe it wasn't worth the wear and tear on my body and the stress on my family for me to keep playing and being unhappy in my hometown. She let me vent. We sat on the phone in silence for a while and then she said, "Okay, if you quit . . . then what?"

I had always wanted to retire on my own terms, not on those terms dictated by someone else. I still had plenty of gas left in the tank. Walking away would've been stupid, and Brandy helped me realize that. I flew back home to Toronto and went straight to the club's offices. That's what they wanted right? Straight to work.

"I'm here. Let's talk contract. You brought me all the way here, so let's sort this out once and for all."

———

The thing about MLS pre-season, which I was never a big fan of, is that you're playing against other MLS teams, and you're basically showing your opposition your hand. In other countries, they may play one or two teams from the same league, but they go abroad and test themselves against other teams that they'll never play during the year. At least Winter understood that and took the team to Turkey.

In past pre-season camps, I would just focus on breathing, blocking out the fans. The mental prep can't be overlooked. Physically, I focused on positioning, opening up my body to turn this way and turn that way. I was there to get my body functioning and to feel things out. When a coach would yell, "Come on!" I would think, "Come on what?" This is pre-season. I'll show you how intense I can get and then ease off. I'm not gonna bust my ass. I wished that 2011 pre-season was that easy. It was really one of the most trying times in my career.

Winter had brought in all these guys from the Netherlands who weren't good enough. You didn't need my experience or my negative mindset at the time to see that this team wasn't good enough to compete in MLS. I felt like I would have to go above and beyond just for us to be competitive in matches, let alone have a competitive season.

To my disappointment, but not to my surprise, the club still hadn't presented me with a fair contract. We had wrapped up a long and emotionally draining camp in Turkey and were back in the States for our final games before kicking off the 2011 season. Management kept dragging out our negotiations, making excuse after excuse.

"We are going to sort this out. We are going to find a solution, just give us some time."

How much time did they need? The season was starting in two weeks. My agent called and had never sounded so defeated.

"DeRo, I am exhausted. These guys have dragged this out longer than I could've ever imagined, and I really don't see a solution. They're not going to come around. I don't know what else to do."

I didn't want to hear that, but it was clear to me that the only thing left to do was play hardball. Despite what was going on off the field, I'd been doing the business and working my ass off with the team in preseason. When I turned up at training the next day, I did something I had never done before in my life.

"Coach. I'm not gonna play. My hamstrings are hurting. I don't think I can play."

I was fed up. Management had played a bunch of stupid tricks on me, now it was my turn, as petty as it was.

We kicked off the 2011 season in Vancouver, their first MLS game. It was a big deal for the country to have two MLS teams. A really special moment for Canadian soccer seemed like the perfect game to be my last for TFC. I told my agent that I would play the season opener and then sit out until they traded me or finally came around and met our price. He hung up the phone and called me right back.

"You know what? Make next week's home opener in Toronto be your last game. The fans deserve it," he said.

"Damn, David, now *you're* the one dragging this shit out!"

He was right though. I told him that's what I would do because he was the one who asked me and he was right about the fans. But to be honest, at that time, I was disappointed that the fans weren't putting more pressure on the club. They knew I was unhappy off the field and that the club was showing special treatment to other guys. I really wanted the fans to go to bat for me and put pressure on TFC to keep me around long term. I didn't want to leave the club. I just wanted to be treated like I was appreciated and valued for what I delivered.

Nick Dasovic defended me when the cheque-signing incident blew up in his face as TFC's interim head coach. He told me management had pressured him to strip me of the captaincy. He told them he wouldn't. Nick knew how much work I had put in and all the bullshit I went through before he became the interim coach. Nick needed me, and I really wanted TFC to give Nick the full-time head-coaching job. He deserved it, and the club deserved a Canadian coach. Instead, they chose the Dutchman with a famous German friend.

My entire life, I let out all my frustrations and all my stress in the game. My parents, school, the streets, whatever was bothering me was released when I was out there on the field. It was my escape. But now, 90 minutes wasn't long enough. Before we flew out to Vancouver to open the 2011 season, my dad told me, "Go out there and don't do nothing. That's what they deserve." He had never said that before. I think he surprised himself. I knew where it came from. He could see how much stress I was under and how hopeless and sad I was that leaving Toronto felt like the best option. I told him I couldn't do that. I was too competitive to do that.

Vancouver was so excited to have an MLS team. The city has a great soccer history, so it was special that they now had a platform to play the best teams in MLS. The vibe in the city was electric. But I blocked out everything on the bus ride to the stadium. I felt like everyone thought I was going to go out there and shit the bed. I didn't let them have that gratification. I was still the captain and I led my team. When the Canadian national anthem played, I found a little more motivation. It was my first time as a pro that only one anthem was sung before kickoff. My anthem. That was special.

Whitecaps fans had the stadium rocking. The sun was shining bright. It was a perfect day. Those fans had been waiting for that moment for years, and they didn't have to wait as long as TFC's fans to see a goal. Eric Hassli scored the first goal in Vancouver's MLS history, 15 minutes into the game. Five minutes later, I tied it up with the 8,000th goal in league history, though I didn't know it at the time. We lost the game 4–2, but if that was going to be the last time I scored in a TFC shirt, at least I left my mark in the history books.

The home opener was the next week. I had told my agent it would be my last game if we couldn't work something out. In my heart, I really thought we would. On the way back from Vancouver, I told Paul Mariner that I wouldn't play another game for the club after the home opener. He really didn't see that coming.

"Dwayne, that can't be. We've got to work something out."

I didn't show up to training. I thought, "Go ahead and fine me. I'm not going to show up." No one from head office called me. It was like nobody cared. If I'm the owner of a club and my star player literally stops showing up for work, you better believe I'm picking up the phone and taking the guy out to talk. "Let's go for coffee. What do we got to do to make things right and get on the same page?"

Paul finally called me on Wednesday.

"Look, I know you're not happy. We're working on something. Stay by your phone."

Stay by my phone? We were playing on Saturday. Were they really going to finish this deal by Friday? So I made some joke about how I didn't think they paid their accountants to work on Fridays on purpose.

"No, we don't want to pay you." He wasn't joking.

I was surprised he let that slip. I really thought Paul was calling because they were trying to work out a way to keep me. They were working on a move to trade me. While I knew that was the most likely outcome, it was still hard to stomach. I had all these dreams of watching my kids grow up in my hometown. When I made the tough choice to leave Houston, I really thought Toronto would be the last club I ever played for. The waiting game was tough. Hours felt like days. Paul called back on Thursday night.

"You're going to be really happy with me."

Oh yeah? You're doing favours for me now? You guys come into my country, my city, make me leave my team, and you think you're doing me a favour?

"New York Red Bulls. We worked out a deal. You can't say anything. They will call you tomorrow. It's unfortunate we couldn't work something out, but I think you'll agree this is the best situation for you. You'll be playing on a top club with top players. You'll probably win the league," he said.

I had never felt so disrespected in my life. Win the league? He really said that to me, like it mattered to me in that moment. On one hand, I was happy to close the chapter on what I knew was over. But on the other hand, now I had a million new things to deal with, just a couple of weeks into the season. Before I even hung up the phone with Paul, I was already thinking about how quickly I'd have to move my family and how the media was going to be all over me. I knew the next few days were going to be hell. Paul asked me to show up to training on Friday. I didn't want to go all the way down there to be their puppet and to be tossed helplessly in front of the media to look like the bad guy in all this. I wasn't the bad guy.

During the two years I played in Toronto, a hundred guys played for TFC. There were six coaches. There was so much turnover. The team would never have found success if they continued to operate that way. Tom Anselmi, president of MLSE at the time, wrote in his book, "Dwayne and Vince Carter, they were like the same," as in, we were self-centred and didn't care about our teams. Not true. I cared so much more because it was my hometown club. Eventually my frustrations took over because I was seeing the same behaviour and poor decisions over and over. Tom never reached out when he was in charge at MLSE. He never offered to take care of me or help us reach an agreement. A quick conversation would've gone a long way. Clubs with fewer resources found creative ways to get around the league's financial restrictions all the time. I thought, "Give me a condo to hold and flip." According to MLS's public salary records, Alessandro Nesta was playing in Montreal on $200,000. You think a legendary World Cup winner would have left A.C. Milan for $200,000 a year?

Bottom line: treat your stars like they're stars. The people in charge at the time didn't do that, and I had to say goodbye to Toronto.

CHAPTER 12

ME AGAINST THE WORLD

I was born kicking. I thought that was just something my parents said because I always had to be dragged to do things I didn't want to. But I fell in love with soccer at a young age and would go happily.

There are a lot of things I don't miss about playing, like the travel, the politics and the bullshit, and the heavy-weight training sessions. I preferred water training, running on the beach or up hills. The older I got, the more my teammates joked about me being that guy who would make every excuse under the sun to get out of weight sessions. But I was always a "less weight, more reps" guy with a push-up, pull-up, and sit-up routine that worked best for me.

The best way to train was on the field. That's where you get completely immersed. It's just you and the ball, in the elements, trying to achieve a particular goal. You tune everything out, and you're just focused on the immediate task. When the session is over, you take a few moments to decompress, and then real life hits you quick. Dad life or husband duties become your focus for the rest of the day. Switching your phone on to see you've missed a million calls is one of the most annoying feelings in the world. Most of the time it's nothing, but when it's not, your world can stop in an instant.

The 2007 season was a real battle in Houston. It's never easy defending a championship; everyone is after you. Repeating is even harder than winning it the first time. Finishing off the regular season strong to put ourselves in the best playoff position possible was my main focus once September hit. Every training session was more intense than the last.

After one long day, I turned my phone on to see I had missed like 50 calls from my brother. Before I could call him back, he called me again. I could hear right away that he was crying.

"Bro, what's going on?"

I had never heard my brother cry like that before. He was with my Aunt Lea. She was not in a good place. "Yo, something's wrong with Auntie Lea, bro. I don't know what it is man. She's sick or something. Something is really wrong bro. I don't know what to do."

There was this deep sadness to his fear. I got on the phone with her, and she didn't know who she was talking to. She was just talking gibberish. It was like her mind was gone. She was in a spiral and couldn't come out of it.

I had to take a trip home to see her. I already knew her health wasn't very good. She got old, very quickly. I was nervous getting on the flight. That short conversation I had with her was haunting me. That wasn't my Aunt Lea. I didn't know who I was going to find when I got back to Toronto. My brother picked me up at the airport. I asked a few questions when I first got in the car, and then I don't think either of us said a word for the rest of the drive.

Seeing her was hard. She had been such a strong woman, and now she was broken with dementia. I spent days thinking about how things used to be and all the sacrifices she made. She didn't have to take my dad and his three boys in. We had a very close relationship, even as she got older. I was her baby. It was hard for me to accept that she was deteriorating.

I went back to Houston and tried to focus on the rest of the season. We kept in contact, but the conversations weren't the same. My brothers helped take care of her and made her comfortable. At MLS Cup, I wanted to give her a lasting memory on her deathbed. I thought about her a lot during the match and shed a few tears thinking of her after we won.

My Auntie Lea died on Christmas Day. I was devastated. I'll never forget that day. As a father, you know it's the most important day of the year for your children, and I knew I had to be strong for my kids and still make Christmas special for them, but I was heartbroken. I think about Auntie every single Christmas. It took years before I could really enjoy Christmas again. The next year was my first in Toronto; I had been traded just a couple of weeks before. We had this great house and could have all my family over, except her.

She never got to see me play for my hometown club. She would have loved that. She would have given me shit for the cheque signing. But she would have absolutely loved watching me play in that red shirt, with a Canadian flag on my arm, because she knew how much it meant to me. And I knew how much Canada meant to her.

That's what I thought about on my final drive to Toronto FC's training ground. I had been traded away. Now that this frustrating chapter was closing, I could look past all the drama and process it as a person. It hurt.

The trade was announced on Friday. I went in just to clean out my locker, then went straight to the airport to fly to New Jersey. It felt so strange to not have an answer when the customs officer asked, "When will you be returning to Canada, sir?"

When you take as many flights as I have, you only remember the wild ones. Sitting down in my seat as an ex-TFC player, I felt a calmness for the first time in a long time. It was my moment to just relax and put all the negativity behind me. I slept almost the entire way, probably with a smile on my face.

I was taken straight to the Red Bulls training ground. The team had pushed back the day's training session so I could get one in with my new teammates before our match the next day, which, funny enough, was against my old Houston Dynamo. I knew I had to hit the ground running — New York was a team that expected to win the MLS Cup. I didn't have any doubt that I could adapt quickly. Walking into the dressing room and seeing the talent I would be playing with got me so excited. I knew I was walking into a winning environment, but it was a different feeling to shake hands with Thierry Henry knowing that he was my teammate. It also meant I couldn't have my No. 14 and had to settle for No. 11. Playing against Rafa Márquez was not fun, but now as teammates, we had the same goals. I felt refuelled.

Pulling that Red Bulls training shirt over my head for the first time made me think of my childhood. I was excited to lace up my boots and hit the pitch with my new teammates. I was joking and laughing with everybody. It reminded me of my days playing for the Malvern Magic and G.S. United. Uncle Dave Sidhu was one of my biggest mentors growing up. He took a lot of us West Indian kids with complicated personalities and backgrounds and created an environment that we felt very comfortable playing in. My dad and Uncle Dave ran our local team for years and, yeah, the game took me to incredible places, but I always missed that feeling. At least for one day, I felt like a kid again. And I really felt wanted.

My whole family was at my first game. I walked into Red Bull Arena with my kids by my side, and that really calmed me. I put so much pressure on myself to perform. I was angry things didn't work out in Toronto and that I had to prove myself again. But I was also excited. And I was ready, even though I had just met my teammates the day before. It was strange to look at the Dynamo during warm-ups and know more players in orange than I did on my own team. And what a stadium. If you were blindfolded on the drive in and didn't know where you were, you would think you were somewhere in Europe, not Harrison, New Jersey. Just the look and the smell of the place made the game feel bigger. Since the renovations, BMO Field feels like that now.

I looked around as the blue seats filled with fans and thought, "I can't wait to get them up off their feet and win them over." Head coach, Hans Backe told me he wanted to get me in as early as he could, and I came on to start the second half. My adrenaline was through the roof, and the fans gave me a nice welcoming. I couldn't wait to get on the ball. My first touch was just behind the halfway line. I turned and looked up to see Dane Richards cutting across the defender. I knew he could run, so I sent him a through ball that he ran right into the back of the net. The whole team ran to the corner flag and mobbed the two of us. "Welcome to New York!" a few guys shouted. It felt really good to be there.

My brother Mark always read the stories written about me or listened for what was said on TV. He'd only share the stuff he felt like I really needed to hear. When my trade from Toronto was announced, NYRB sporting director Erik Solér said, "Dwayne has been one of the league's best players over the past several years, and we are thrilled that he is a Red Bull. He is one of the most dangerous players MLS has seen in the attacking third, and he is a true leader both on and off the field. We think this is a massive step in our quest towards the MLS Cup title."

That showed me that New York valued me right away, and they continued to show that with all the little things they did for me. They sent a car to pick me up for every appearance, arranged travel, and made sure my family was always taken care of. Everything was professional. The team had just committed to be the first MLS team to play Arsenal and PSG in the Emirates Cup that upcoming summer. New York operated in a different league, and all I could think was, "Fuck, this is what I wanted in my city. Why wasn't it like this at TFC?"

I'd asked TFC to give me my own suite. I'm old enough — I don't need a roommate. In New York, they gave it to me automatically. When we checked in, I asked the team rep, "I don't have a roommate on this trip?" He laughed. "No, of course not. You'll always have your own room. Thierry, Rafa, Teemu Pukki, and you all get your own suites on the road. And you fly first class on all our trips."

I liked the way they thought.

That's how it should be. It makes you feel good. It makes you want to be there. And on the soccer side, we had the pieces to win. New York was the best team in the Eastern Conference the year before, but they were knocked out in the first round of the playoffs. I could feel the team was motivated by that failure. Plus, with a brand new stadium, there was a lot of pressure to deliver in the second season at Red Bull Arena. Making the trade for me showed how bad they wanted to avoid an early playoff exit again.

Toronto FC picked up Danleigh Borman and Tony Tchani in the trade. Neither of those guys lasted the whole season. All Aron Winter wanted was young guys. He had this big vision and long-term plan for TFC. I told him in pre-season, "Bro, just focus on this year. Get experience. Experience is what's gonna win in this league. Surround the experienced players with young guns. Because, yes, young players are the future — I'm not knocking that — but experience is what wins championships in MLS. Let the young guys learn off of them and then put one or two young kids into the mix. Inject them here and there so they can learn the game, not have them carry the load."

Winter had a bunch of young players in Toronto that didn't understand the game. When the going gets tough, kids don't know what the hell to do. I had a lot of friends in that dressing room and cared so much about the club, I kept a close eye on things from New York. It was hard watching TFC struggle and fall apart on the pitch while my Red Bulls were winning games and growing into something special. Especially because TFC and a lot of fans had branded me a traitor. All I could think was, "Why did it have to be like this?"

I didn't want to talk to anyone from Toronto. Maybe that made it easy for the media to hate on me. Everyone was hitting me up, trying to get my side of the story. But I wasn't ready to tell it for the longest time. I don't know if I felt like they had already made up their minds and didn't deserve to hear it, or if rehashing it would've prevented me from moving forward with my game and my life. My best interview was with Gareth Wheeler on *The Grill Room*, a Toronto sports TV show. That was the first time I really expressed myself. Tim Micallef and Sid Seixeiro on Sportsnet supported me too, so I had some supporters back home. But it felt like the average soccer fan thought that I was the bad guy.

The average fan can't relate to the player because they see the dollar figure and think the player is just being selfish. But they come and pay their money to watch me play and watch me perform and see that they're getting their money's worth. When I came back to Toronto, a lot of fans told me, "You produced the whole time, and the team didn't take care of you. If you weren't performing, we'd have hated you. But you didn't. We miss you, man."

Money makes the world go round. New York was paying a lot of guys a lot of money for appearances. That's how clubs get around the salary cap restrictions. I don't think the Red Bulls knew all the details of my TFC contract and what I was getting paid for appearances. Taking on my deal put New York over the cap — they had too many high-priced guys. I knew they were going to have to make another move to make it all work. I thought they were going to trade Teemu.

We were getting results and had the whole league talking about us. The schedule had us on the road a lot, which helped me get to know the guys even better and really settle in. We flew out to Los Angeles to play Beckham, Landon Donovan, and the Galaxy, and the hype train was like an MLS Cup Final. "A star-studded summer blockbuster featuring the league's two richest teams," the headlines read. The next week I scored my first goal as a Red Bull, against Chivas USA, though that night was spoiled with a loss. But everything was building. And then the 2011 Gold Cup ramped up and took five of us away from the team.

The tournament totally disrupts the MLS season. It's really unfair to the fans and the players. That Gold Cup was really frustrating for me. We lost our big showdown in Detroit against the United States, barely beat Guadeloupe in Tampa, and then fell apart late against Panama. Canada didn't even make the knockout round. Another national team disappointment. I was happy to get back to New York and focus on the season. Five days after the Panama game, we were in Portland. The Timbers had us running around chasing shadows. We were losing 3–1 with 20 minutes left. Henry scored and then got a red card late in the game. I stepped up and drilled home a penalty in the 96th minute to take the point for us. It was wild.

We were underperforming that month and drew a bunch of games. It weighed on me because I had a lot going on. After I got traded to

New York, it took time to tie everything up in Toronto. The kids had just a couple months of school left, so we decided they'd come join me in New Jersey at the end of June. My daughter was graduating elementary school, and I wasn't going to mess with that. Brandy handled everything. She sold the house in Oakville and dealt with real estate agents for weeks picking out a place in New Jersey. I scoped out a few spots before we made our decision, but she had done all the research and hard work. She always did.

Our schedule worked out so I had a break to fly home to be there for my daughter's graduation. It was really going to be the perfect way for all of us to say goodbye to Toronto. And, finally, I could help Brandy with the move. I remember that training session before the break so clearly. It was a Monday afternoon. I was going to fly out first thing in the morning to be there for the graduation, and then we would make the journey to New Jersey together. I was intense in every training session, but there was a little bit more to me that day. I think I just wanted to leave it all out there so I could head off. Training finished and I rushed home. I remember putting the key in the door and thinking, "This is the last time it will be quiet when I get home." The time couldn't go by fast enough. I made myself one big meal and started packing my duffle bag for the flight to Toronto, when my phone rang. It was Thierry.

"DeRo, did you see the website? You just got traded."

What the fuck?

"This is bullshit! Who is gonna fucking feed me the balls?" he said angrily.

I was in shock. "Bro, you have power. Couldn't you have told them not to make this move?"

"They didn't tell me about this! No one talked to me about this!" he said.

We had a real partnership on the field, and we were friends off of it. He knew I was living by myself and sad to be away from my family and would drive out to Hoboken to take me out for lunch all the time. Thierry was a great friend to have on your team. I couldn't believe I was hearing the news from him, and not Hans. I was just in the office a few hours earlier. It seemed like a sick joke. I had just got there. I had played just 13 games. My family was all packed up and ready to move into the empty house I had been living in — the moving truck was literally sitting in the driveway in Oakville ahead of our 10-hour drive the next day.

I called my agent. The first thing he said was, "I'm done with this league. I don't want anything to do with this league anymore."

David Baldwin worked with a lot of top players in Europe. The way sports teams operate in North America was so foreign to him. He'd had enough. And I had to figure out how the hell I was going to break the news to my wife. "Hey, about all that hard work . . . well, it was a waste. I just got traded to D.C."

I just sat and stared at my phone for the longest time. I knew she was in Mississauga, watching my son's soccer game.

"Hey, I know you're at the game . . ."

"Yeah, they're doing good right now. What's up?"

I told her to get up and go for a walk. She sounded annoyed, like she knew something was wrong and that she would have to fix it.

"I got traded."

I could hear the shock through the phone. And then came the tears.

That was the first time I felt lower than low. I was thinking to myself, "Fuck, how did this happen?" First TFC, now New York. I never wanted to be that player who got traded here, there, and everywhere. New York didn't work out financially, and now I was leaving again. How would this affect my image? And Brandy was thinking about all the work she'd already done and all the work she had to undo. That's stress man. She had to call the moving company and make them drive our stuff to a holding facility, hoping we'd be able to make a full move to D.C. in the coming weeks. It was an awful situation to be in.

To their credit, the Red Bulls stepped up and made everything right with the family move to D.C. But I was pissed at Hans for not being upfront with me. He could've handled everything better. He knew I was settling down and buying a place and that I saw myself as a key part of the team. I thought I was going to be a Red Bull for a long time, and he knew that. I went to the stadium to say my goodbyes and get my things. I saw Hans and the first thing he said was, "I'm sorry."

"It's done. Nothing to talk about. You did what you felt like you needed to do. Have a good season, y'all. I'm out," I replied, and left.

—

The trade didn't make sense to anybody. Hans and Erik were roasted by the fans and the media for only getting Dax McCarty back in exchange. It was just a business move to them. Dax wasn't making as much money against the cap. But it felt shitty to be treated as disposable.

Life had come full circle. My first taste of MLS life had been with D.C. United, on that trip to El Salvador with Frank Yallop. If he hadn't left for San Jose, I would've signed with D.C. Who knows what might've happened? Maybe I would have won four MLS Cups with D.C. United? Maybe not.

Here I was, 11 years later, pulling on that D.C. United shirt, for real. And this was not the team I trained with as a 22-year-old. There weren't any guys like Jaime Moreno and Marco Etcheverry on this team. I was the old guy now.

I got to wear No. 7 again. A lot of people don't know, but that was my original number. I wore No. 7 growing up and only switched to No. 14 as a pro because No. 7 wasn't available. I doubled it up because I wanted to put in double the effort of whoever was wearing No. 7 at the time.

D.C. United was a young team, with a young coach in Ben Olsen, hoping to rebuild on the fly and get back to the top. I wasn't the only Canadian. Dejan Jakovic had left Red Star Belgrade and joined D.C. United the year before. My old friend Pat Onstad had been named goal-keeping coach at the start of the season. It was nice to have two familiar faces in the locker room that first day. Now I had to develop this under-standing with a brand new team all over again. That takes time to develop.

In New York, we had more players who could adapt in a shorter period. D.C. was a team of talented, hungry, young guys still learning on the job. These guys wanted to listen and learn, and they looked up to me right away. They played carefree because they wanted to prove themselves. There's a fearlessness that makes young players dangerous. That was exciting. And so was the schedule.

You can call it fate or you can call it coincidence, but I know it was good fortune that my second game in black and red was against the Red Bulls. I wanted to show them how big of a mistake they had made by trading me away. I wasn't there very long, but I grew to like a lot of those players. As soon as the referee blew the whistle though, it was war.

New York versus D.C. was one of the first big rivalries in MLS. It means a lot to the fans when you can stick it to the other team. I told my teammates in the locker room that there was no way we were going to lose the game. New York was flying high, coming off a big win the week before. They moved the ball really well, looking to expose our inexperienced players. But then I saw my chance. My teammate Josh Wolff was a few feet behind me as the ball was poked my way. I stepped over it and dummied the defender, then sprinted by him. Josh fed me a great pass; I took one touch and smashed it past Greg Sutton. I didn't do my shake 'n bake celebration for some reason. I just punched the air one time and yelled as loud as I could. The Red Bulls were pissed that it was me who scored. I could see it on their faces. My new teammates mobbed me, and we hung on for the 1–0 win.

At the end of the game, Thierry came up and said, "I was afraid you were going to do something like that."

I stared down Hans as I walked off. He said something to me, but I wasn't hearing anything. Those were a sweet-tasting three points.

I had a brand new motivation at D.C. When I got traded, I told myself that I was going to light up the league. I went out there every game, looking to score at least two goals. That didn't happen, but I made a habit of scoring. I netted the fastest first-half hat trick in MLS history against Real Salt Lake: nine minutes. But my most satisfying goals at RFK were against TFC.

When they first handed me the schedule, I circled Toronto's visit. I'd had just over a month with my new team. We were still learning each other's tendencies and gelling as a unit. But with Josh Wolff and Charlie

Davies playing in front of me, we were a threat to score every time we had the ball in an opponent's zone. My whole team knew how badly I wanted to show up TFC. There was a "Do it for DeRo" attitude leading up to the game.

That morning, I woke up wanting to kick their asses. I wasn't going to come off that field without doing something special. It may have just looked like another game in the middle of the season, but that night it meant so much more to both sides. I knew TFC wanted to shut me down. They weren't about to let me embarrass them.

The whole game was ridiculous. Jasen Anno was the referee. He sent off our goalkeeper Bill Hamid in the seventh minute. You rarely see that in MLS. Hamid came out and took down Eric Avila outside the box. Avila somersaulted through the air and made it look way more dramatic than it was. Just like that, we were down to 10 men, and our backup keeper, Steve Cronin, had to come in cold. Every time I played against my old teams, something weird happened. Maybe it was the universe's way of testing me: Are you prepared for this? Are you ready to elevate your game and face adversity?

Recognizing when it's your moment is the key to everything in life. We had a free kick inside the halfway line and sent the defenders forward into the box, leaving TFC bracing for a big cross in. I didn't crash the box and just floated until they didn't see me as a threat. Then I sprinted towards the crowded box and got fed the ball on my right foot. I hit a rocket from 25 yards out into the low corner. 1–0 good guys.

The week of the game, everyone asked me how I would celebrate if I scored against Toronto. When I saw the ball go in, I just put my hand on my heart and turned around to walk back for the restart. I was jacked up to score against them, but I wanted to be respectful to the TFC fans who had shown me so much love when I was a Red.

I got a kick out of watching Aron Winter and his assistants, Paul Mariner and Bob de Klerk, lose it on the sidelines. They were pissed. Apparently, the talk in the room before the game was, "Don't let DeRo score. He's gonna be hungry tonight. Shut him down." I heard that de Klerk was the angriest of all three of them. At halftime, he kicked a rolling cart in the middle of the room and something flew off of it and hit Doneil Henry in the face.

There was a different edge to the second half. Toronto's players were even more physical towards me. My buddy Julian de Guzman was shoving me and trying to play me extra hard. He really wanted to stop me, but he knew he couldn't. I was a man possessed, and there was nothing he could do about it. Winter and Mariner were hard on him in the locker room. He was the captain now and the highest paid guy, so he was getting all the pressure from the coaching staff.

As physical as TFC were, I could sense a nervousness. My teammate Chris Pontius swung a ball into the box that had no business getting to me, but it went right through TFC defender Andy Iro, like he wasn't even there. I couldn't believe the ball ended up at my feet. I reacted quickly, stepped around a sprawling Stefan Frei and made it 2–1. Can't make mistakes like that around me. I still didn't celebrate, but I couldn't resist hyping up our D.C. United fans a little bit. The Screaming Eagles and Barra Brava were very good to me in D.C.

A few minutes after I scored to put us in front, Julian hit a screamer from 100 yards out to tie the game 2–2. Okay, it was probably 30 yards, but I had never seen him score a goal like that. It was his first goal in a TFC shirt. I know that was something he had wanted for a very long time, and he was feeling a lot of pressure to finally score. But I was cheesed that he had to do it against my team. We're very good friends, but were enemies during a match. After the game I complimented him on his goal and told him, "Nice to see you taking notes from me."

Just before Julian scored, something weird happened. Ben Olsen wanted to make a substitution to bring on Ethan White, but the ball had gone out for a throw in. He wasn't in position to enter the pitch, but referee Jasen Anno waved him on. White went flying in but Anno gave TFC the green light before our defender got in position — something that's just not done — leaving Julian with loads of space to burn us. I definitely didn't hear a whistle and neither did my teammates. Ben totally lost it. He stormed the field and was yelling his head off. I would've done the same if I was coaching that day. Ben was ejected, leaving us without our starting keeper and our head coach.

TFC hadn't won a game on the road all season. They took the lead in the 87th minute off a corner kick, when we had fallen asleep at the back. I was so pissed. I didn't expect TFC to roll over for us, but I sure as hell wasn't going to let them win on my turf. Just my luck, less than a minute later, we marched down the pitch, building an attack, and poor Andy Iro, again, knocked over United's Austin da Luz in the box. I don't even know if Anno pointed to the penalty spot before I was looking for the ball to take the shot. I was laser focused; I couldn't hear a sound in the entire stadium. Stefan leaned to his right, and I put it into the left side of his net for my hat trick: 3–3, final score.

It was one of the craziest games of my entire career. I took a lot of satisfaction knowing that Winter and Mariner walked away upset that their team couldn't stop me. They brought it on themselves, though. I don't believe in shit-talking before a game. Your actions should do the talking. And man, did they ever that night. But I was mad that we took only one point. We really needed every point we could get in order to make the playoffs. I couldn't afford to go another year without at least a chance at an MLS Cup run.

I called my dad after the game. He was thrilled.

"You showed them! The hell with the dropped points. You showed them they shouldn't have traded you!"

Torsten Frings was Toronto's big summer signing. He came up to me after the game and said, "I don't know what this team was thinking to let you go. They want me to score goals. I'm a defensive midfielder. It's crazy over here!"

Having a World Cup player show me that respect meant a lot to me. I was envious that Julian got to practise and train with him every day. I would have loved that chance. I told Torsten, "Listen, bro, that's my city. Unfortunately, it is what it is. It would've been an honour to play with you. I see they got you running all over the place, scoring goals when you're not a goal scorer. I feel for you."

D.C. United missed the playoffs. It was such a shitty feeling. We were so close. I wanted another championship, and I wanted to do it with this team of underdogs. Maybe if Toronto had traded me to D.C. in April, the season would've been different. Who knows? The universe had other plans to cap my whirlwind year.

CHAPTER 13

WHAT DOESN'T KILL YOU MAKES YOU STRONGER

Maybe I left Houston too early. Maybe if I had gone to Toronto later in my career, things would've been different. Maybe we would have won more championships in Houston? Maybe I wouldn't have left Toronto in such a toxic way?

Leaving my hometown was one of the lowest points of my life. I felt like one man against the city. The people at TFC at that time didn't have the same intentions or the same goals as me. The player turnover, the coaching changes, the back and forth with Mo Johnston, and the general uncertainty drove me nuts. I wasn't willing to stand aside and take it. The Celtic experience was the final nail in the coffin and was really what changed my career path.

My personal production rate took off when I got to D.C. I had a mutual agreement with most of my teammates: when you see me, give me the ball and keep moving. Trust that I'm going to give it back to you. I needed to establish myself in a young team and show them I could lead them. Plus, I needed to show the teams that discarded me what they were missing.

Ben Olsen allowed me to play higher up the pitch and play more instinctively, which I was the most comfortable with. Playing against him for years, I always had a great respect for Ben's tenacity. He never gave up, and he always worked very hard. That attitude can take you a lot of places, and the way he transitioned from being a player to the head coach in just one year was impressive. I knew as soon as I got there that they had a young exciting team in D.C. And with my old friend Pat Onstad part of the coaching staff, I felt very comfortable very quickly. With all the turmoil I had gone through that season, the transition to my third team was a lot easier than I was expecting.

I refused to play in the All-Star Game that year. It had nothing to do with the fans or the league, but everything to do with the coach. I never wanted to play for Hans Backe again. It had been only a month since the trade. The breakup was still too fresh for me, and I didn't want to make him look good against Manchester United. He didn't deserve it. The game was at Red Bull Arena, so it really was a showcase piece for the New York Red Bulls. But if they didn't want me to be a part of their team, I wasn't going to play for their coach. Simple as that.

All the negativity in 2011 was motivation for me on the pitch. I didn't feel supported in Toronto. New York treated me as though I was disposable. All that intensity came out in D.C. I finally won the Golden Boot, with 16 goals and 12 assists in 33 games that year.

I had been runner-up for MLS MVP two times before. Taylor Twellman won the award in 2005, and D.C. United's Christian Gomez beat me to it the very next year. I felt like I didn't have the support campaign behind me like they did. In 2011, D.C. United didn't make the playoffs, and I had played on three teams in one season! That just doesn't happen. Those two factors alone seemed like reason enough for the league to want to give the MVP Award to someone else.

Without the MLS Playoffs to worry about, my focus was solely on the national team. Being in a World Cup Qualifying group with Puerto Rico, Saint Lucia, and St. Kitts and Nevis gave me a chance to unwind and relax my mind in an exotic location, even if just for a few moments.

We were flying back after a disappointing draw in St. Kitts when I got a phone call from Todd Durbin at the league offices.

"Dwayne, I'm pleased to inform you that you've been named 2011 MLS MVP. Congratulations on an incredible year."

At first I thought it was a joke.

I was mad about the St. Kitts game.

I was mad about missing the playoffs.

I really was in shock that after the wildest year of my life, this award that had eluded me all these years was now mine. Was this really happening? Todd sounded way too serious for it to have been a joke. I started balling. To this day, I still get emotional thinking about that phone call.

I was so exhausted emotionally, physically, and mentally when Toronto traded me away. I accepted it when New York said I had to go. My career had always been about difficulties: my turbulent time in Germany, turning down a contract with A.C. Milan, getting cut from the national team at 14. Those situations always inspired me to keep working. Winning one championship wasn't enough. Winning four wasn't enough. I never got complacent. Having that mentality is what made missing the playoffs so painful. But having that mentality meant I was suppressing so many feelings.

Hearing "You've been named MVP" hit me so hard because I immediately thought about all of the people who fought against me and hated on me because they didn't know my situation that year. Fighting with clubs, not knowing I was getting traded, waking up to phone calls telling me I've been dealt again, trying to keep a level head, all while keeping my family intact.

That year was an emotional roller coaster for me on so many levels and largely because it was also draining on everyone around me. Brandy had to quarterback two major moves, get the kids settled, and try to find a life for herself in a new place that we might leave again in just a few months. My kids were uprooted and had to leave their friends behind. My parents were getting so much heat as everyone they knew tried to find out what was going on. My dad couldn't walk around town without someone stopping to give him their hot take on what had happened with TFC or comment on my success with my new team. Same with my brothers. That level of exhaustion really wears on a person. I felt guilty that I could only do so little to deflect that stress off them. There was so much they had to deal with on their own.

My dad was the first person I told. He was more excited than I was. While he was passionate about football, he was not really an emotional guy — didn't get too high or too low — but I could hear in his voice how excited he was. He may have even been a little teary eyed.

It was important to me that my family felt like my award belonged to them. Brandy and the kids each played a part in me reaching the top that season, and I wanted them to be in every photograph with me. We had fun picking out the clothes they wore to the event, and Zegna made me a custom suit. It wasn't as flashy as my introductory press conference suit in Toronto, but it was a boss suit.

The MLS Awards Gala was in L.A. during MLS Cup weekend. Galaxy and Dynamo were in the final. I did feel a little empty getting the biggest individual award at the final and not playing in it. Being in that environment as a spectator sucked. In New York, I truly felt we would have won the MLS Cup if they hadn't traded me. I was starting to understand Henry, and he understood me. Rafa Márquez knew what quality he had in front of him. We were just starting to come together as an entire unit and get to know each other. But it wasn't meant to be, and I had to remind myself that blessings don't always come the way you expect them to.

I was the first person in sports history to get traded twice in the same season, score for three different teams, and win league MVP. When I was presented with the trophy, I was proud of myself. To me, that was the highlight of my MLS career because of everything I had overcome. That trophy was the physical manifestation of all the struggle and strife that I had to overcome to reach that accomplishment. God and the universe work in mysterious ways.

But holding the trophy on that stage was bittersweet. I felt like I should've been standing there in Toronto FC colours. I wished I had been able to bring that individual success to my hometown team. Had the club, Winter, and I worked out our differences, who knows what would've happened. I may have scored 20 goals for TFC. Or I might've fought somebody.

D.C. United rewarded me with a designated player contract. Ben Olsen really fought for me to get that deal, and I thanked him for that.

"You saved my job. I've never seen anybody do what you did this season. You put this team on your back and carried us to the edge of the playoffs," he told me.

It's wild that it took all that to finally get that DP recognition. To me, it wasn't because I had a good 2011 season, but because I consistently improved my body of work. It took this long for me to really feel rewarded for it. I've always held this league at a high standard and respected that we needed to have a good showing in every big test, every All-Star Game, every Champions League game. I put a lot of pressure on myself to show up and represent in those games.

Was I mad MLS didn't step up sooner? Yes. I know it's a business, and I understood the importance of bringing in guys like Beckham, Henry, Angel, and, later, guys like Didier Drogba, Steven Gerrard, and Sebastian Giovinco. But the grinders and the OGs who really built this league weren't rewarded like that. Someone like Eddie Pope, who captained the U.S. National Team, and as a Black man, deserved more respect as a player. There are countless examples of foundation-building guys who were just too early to get theirs.

I'm happy to see how many Canadian and American designated players there are now. It shows the evolution of the league. I do think in 5 to 10 years, MLS will be the number one league in the world. The structure works, and it's only going to get bigger. Sustainable growth has always been a major focus, and these clubs and leagues overseas don't operate that way. I'd still like to see Canadians as the true faces of TFC, the Whitecaps, and the Impact. But it's all part of the evolution process.

We don't promote our Canadian stars. That's not just a soccer thing, but a cultural thing. Our musicians have to make it big in the States first.

Our actors move to L.A., and people think they're American. Christine Sinclair is soccer's all-time leading international goal scorer. She should have a billboard up in Yonge-Dundas Square in downtown Toronto every day, not just when the Women's World Cup comes around. When my kids walk into the Nike store, I want them to look up and see a giant poster of Alphonso Davies, not Neymar or Cristiano Ronaldo. There should be a floor to ceiling portrait of R.J. Barrett or Jamal Murray on the wall, not LeBron James. When big brands make commercials to air in Canada, *our* guys should be in it. They should be the first ones getting the phone call. We don't get that marketing in this country because we as Canadians are too worried about what everybody else is doing. We don't celebrate our own. Atiba Hutchinson is the first Canadian to captain a Champions League game, and nobody knows. Doesn't even make the highlight shows most matchdays.

I've been to so many awards dinners where we would pat ourselves on the backs and nobody saw it. It wasn't on the sports channels or even on the local cable channel. Or if it was, it wasn't being promoted. They presented Joe Fletcher with an award for having refereed the World Cup in Brazil in 2014. He was the first Canadian to do that. That's a big deal. The man went to Russia and officiated the 2018 World Cup too. This is a Canadian doing major things in our sport, and he should be celebrated in a major way for it. He's an example for all Canadian kids, especially Black kids, who see the world ignoring Canadian soccer because we haven't performed on the field.

This man is officiating some of the biggest games in the sport. Let's tell his story so people can see him, can learn about what he's doing in the game while proudly wearing a Canadian flag everywhere he goes. Most soccer fans didn't know he was officiating the World Cup in Brazil until Chile versus Spain, when the cameras caught him in the tunnel before the match, expecting a handshake from some FIFA suit, but the guy completely ignored him and walked onto the other side of the line. Fletch smoothly raised his outstretched hand and rubbed his bald head, to the amusement of Spain's goalkeeper Iker Casillas, who saw the whole thing. The TV shows laughed that up over and over: "Look, Canada is at the World Cup! And just as you'd expect, they get ignored." I saw that and thought, "Wow, that's how we introduce the country to the greatness this man has achieved in our game?"

That's the state that we're in as Canadians; we're just mediocre and the world doesn't take us seriously. Because we don't take ourselves seriously. Fletcher's introduction to his fellow Canadians watching from home should have been with a camera following him up and down the touchline in his first game. And then, sure, you can laugh at that missed handshake. But that can't be the only acknowledgement he gets during the tournament —a moment most people would be embarrassed about for the rest of their lives if it happened to them on worldwide television.

Lots of people think of Brazil as the greatest soccer nation on earth. Brazil gave the world Pelé, Joga bonito, and that iconic yellow shirt pictured in so many of the game's biggest moments. Playing for Canada in a World Cup was my dream. Playing in what could have been my *only* World Cup in *Brazil* would've been a dream come true.

The 2014 World Cup was the last chance for a special generation of Canadian players to play in the world's biggest event. We put ourselves in a great position to reach CONCACAF's final stage of World Cup Qualifying after beating Panama 1–0 in Toronto, thanks to my match-winning goal. Four days later we were down in Panama City, looking to pull off the double, which would've all but guaranteed us a place in The Hex.

There was a lot of emotion on that trip. We could taste how close we were. The focus was as sharp as I'd seen in years. The day before the match, I tried to relax a bit at training. Physically, I was in a great place. And mentally, I was strong and ready for the task at hand. At the end of the session, there was a crowd of fans waiting near the team bus. There will always be autograph hunters, even in a hostile environment. I shook hands with a fan as I walked past him and got a strange vibe when we connected. He had a strange look on his face, almost sinister. When I stepped on the bus, I noticed something on my hand. It looked like dirt, so I wiped my hand on my pants. I distinctly remember thinking how weird that was.

We got back to the hotel and settled in for the night. The Panamanian fans were raging outside. They had the bikes revving and the fireworks going. They were making noise all night long. Some guys take sleeping pills. I liked to fall asleep to music when all that was happening outside. Or meditate. I liked to be in a visualization state of mind the night before a game. But this night, I couldn't.

My mind wasn't at ease. I couldn't stop thinking about that fan and the mark left on my hand. When I got out of bed, my legs felt heavy and I felt lethargic. It was the worst sleep. At breakfast, I was angry at myself for not getting the rest I wanted. But it was game day, so I blocked everything out and focused on the task at hand.

I really felt we had a team to compete. It was our time to do it. Making the final round of World Cup Qualifying had always been such a hurdle. Just getting there would open a new world of possibilities.

The stadium sounded full when the team bus rolled in. Most of Central America does a great job making those grounds feel as intimidating as possible for the visiting teams. From turning off the hot water, or cranking up the heat, or removing the insulation from the walls so you can feel everything and fear the roof might cave in. But we had a real confidence that night. In my mind, this was the game I was going to carry everyone through. I was so hungry that game. I knew we were going to win.

We started all right, unfazed by the crowd and how hyped up the Panama players were. Five minutes into the game, I got the ball in the corner, and just as I turned, the defender stepped down hard on my foot. I went down and knew something didn't feel right. When I stood up, I was in trouble. Then the stadium lights went out. The game stopped. I got to the halfway line and I said to head coach Stephen Hart, "I think I'm done. My leg is messed up. Tape it and let me try." You could see in his eyes, he didn't want to believe it.

The trainer taped me up so I could try to run on it. The lights were still off. I don't know if the Panamanian team or the crowd had any idea of how much pain I was in. When I ran, my leg felt all wobbly, like it wasn't attached to my body. Nearly 15 minutes had passed. As soon as I sat down, admitting defeat to myself and knowing it was too serious to continue, the lights came back on. I was subbed out of the game.

I can still see the faces of the training staff that night. They knew it was bad. There was so much motion when they moved my ankle and knee around. The trainer looked up at me and said, "I'm sorry, I don't know what it is, but it could be a serious knee injury." Hearing that was worse than if it had just been a broken leg. Then at least I would know what was coming.

When I was injured, I was helpless. I tried to stay positive and cheer the guys on from the bench. But I was crushed. I couldn't believe this was how I was going to go out. We lost 2–0, which meant reaching The Hex would come down to our last game, in Honduras. I knew I wouldn't be able to play in that game — I didn't even know if I'd ever be able to play again!

I didn't want to be sitting at home watching that game on my computer. If we were going to crash out and not qualify, I wanted to be there with them. I wanted to be there on the field with my team, my soldiers. That's all I could think about on the bus. I got to the hotel and just sat in my room and cried. I didn't talk to anyone; I didn't want to see anyone — not even my wife or my dad. I couldn't talk to anyone. I just lay there on the bed, crying. I'd occasionally get up and put some Bob Marley on, but then a wave would come over me, and I'd just start crying again. All night.

I felt like I let the country down. I let myself down. The trip back to Toronto was just a painful journey, physically and emotionally. It was the worst flight of my life. Brandy came to my doctor's appointment with me. "This might be the end of my career," I told her on the drive over.

"Dwayne, I'm sorry, but as you may already know, you're going to be out for a while," the doctor said.

Thankfully, it wasn't career ending, but I thought my season was done. That hurt in a whole different way because we had something special brewing at D.C. United. The guys finished the regular season strong and went into the playoffs with a real chance to make a run.

D.C. United met New York in the playoffs a couple of months later. That was such a wild time. Hurricane Sandy had wreaked havoc on the

East Coast and messed with our schedule. D.C. finished higher in the standings in the regular season and should have hosted the second leg, but instead they reversed the order and had us open at home.

The playoff format at the time allowed for potential conference crossover, and Houston had beat Chicago in the wildcard game, pitting them against us in the Eastern Conference Final. When I saw that, I knew they were going to be a problem for us. Houston just got better as the playoffs went on and came out on fire in the first leg. They were so hungry, and D.C. just couldn't recover. It hurt so bad to not be out there. It always killed me to sit there helpless, while my guys fought without me. But this stung more.

I was working so hard to get back on the field before the end of the season. By the grace of God, I got the doctor's clearance to dress for the second game against Houston. My leg was taped up from top to bottom. Looking back on it, I can't believe I was able to play two months after the injury in Panama. Ben knew how badly I wanted to be out there and subbed me into the game with about half an hour to play. The crowd roared. That took away any of the pain I was feeling. I was definitely running on will and adrenaline, hoping I could make the impact we needed to keep our season alive. We lost and as hard as that was for me to stomach, at 34, I was afraid I would never get another chance to play for a championship, or even score another goal.

———

It's not a coincidence that big moments in my career came against the teams that gave up on me. I strongly believe that. I was stuck on 99 MLS goals for a little bit in 2012, but I had a feeling that would change after seeing New York on the schedule. It was the end of the summer — just a couple of weeks before that awful night in Panama — and we couldn't afford to keep dropping points. We had really started to find our groove and needed to rack up wins to grab a playoff spot.

Tim Cahill was New York's big-money signing that season. Thierry Henry needed someone to feed him the ball, so they spent the money on another Premier League star. I wanted to show them it should've been me. I was so hyped that night, I didn't even look to pass the ball off the kickoff. I just took it and started running forward. Cahill had a big chance a few minutes into the game when Henry sent a big free kick into the box, laser-targeted for Cahill's head. I held my breath for a second, but Bill Hamid made the perfect save.

New York did score first when Thierry stretched out like he was making a slide tackle to put the ball into space for Joel Lindpere. He blasted it by Bill. We were game for a fight that night though. New York couldn't clear the ball and it fell to me at the top of the box. I could see Nick DeLeon making a run into the box, so I just floated the ball towards him. He didn't connect cleanly but did just enough to direct it past the goalkeeper. Nick turned around and pointed at me with the biggest smile on his face. It wasn't too often I was behind him to set him up. At halftime I said to him, "Nice work. Now you owe me a goal."

Sure enough in the second half, Nick got the ball behind the halfway line and looked up to see me at the top of the line, with a step on my defender. He launched the ball forward and made me run for it. I could see the keeper charging out towards me. Bill Gaudette was a big guy. I knew it was a gamble to connect with the ball. I could've been knocked out or had my ribs broken. I thought, "I'm either gonna wake up in the morning and ask 'what happened?' or I'm going to score number 100 here." I really thought Gaudette was going to crush me. But instead, somehow, he pulled out. I got my head on it and directed it by him. I gave an extended shake 'n bake celebration after that one. Thierry Henry had the biggest smile on his face when I passed by him.

"My man, congrats."

That felt really nice. Here's a guy I didn't play with for very long, but I left an impression on. He saw the work I put in and knew the bullshit I had gone through. It was a relief to finally reach 100, and it was a special landmark. I had played the majority of my career as an attacking midfielder, so to join the century club and put my name in the history books with guys who had mainly played as centre-forwards was special. After

I scored 100, I was gunning for Jaime Moreno and Landon's record. I wanted 150, as unrealistic as it was.

The thought of scoring again and sending the crowd into a frenzy is what motivated me through rehab that off-season. I wasn't going to let the injury be the end of my story. Getting ready for the start of 2013 was hell. I pushed myself to extremes to overcome that setback. I had high hopes for myself and the team, but it was such a wildly frustrating season. We won just three league games — the lowest win total in MLS history. Somehow, we found enough magic to win the US Open Cup title, which meant we had qualified for the CONCACAF Champions League, but that didn't stop ownership from wanting to rebuild. And I wasn't part of their plans.

They had workers ripping down my giant banner on the side of the stadium before I even left the parking lot on my last day. That's how quickly things move in professional sports. "Okay, thank you. On to the next one." I had no idea what that meant for me. I had offers to go to Mexico. But I was exhausted. My kids were too. My wife had handled all the moves because I was always away, and I know that weight took its toll. So I was kind of surprised when Brandy told me, "I got one more big move left in me, so if Mexico is what you want, let's do it."

I didn't want to. I had moved my family all over, I didn't want to do it again. I didn't want to bring them down to Mexico and I didn't want to be away from them. If it was a two or three-year offer, I may have considered going, but the prospect of being away just wasn't appealing anymore.

My kids were getting to that age where they were attached to their phones. I made a point, or at least tried, to not use mine when I was sat at the dinner table with them. I wasn't always good at that. One day, I sat down with my phone in my pocket and was surprised when it rang. I pulled it out to send the call to my voicemail, but I noticed the call was coming from a Toronto-area number that I didn't recognize. Surprised, I answered the phone and heard a very distinguished voice on the other end.

"Dwayne! What's going on man! Are you ready to come home to Toronto?"

"Excuse me?" I asked, very confused. I was trying to figure out who this stranger was. It was Tim Leiweke. Everything this man touched turned to gold. He was a very important person in the Los Angeles sports scene, and when he had become CEO of MLSE, I knew he was going to make big changes to their organizations. He manifests greatness.

"Dwayne, we're building something here. And we want you to be a part of it. You're important to this team, now and in the future."

I wasn't too sure going back was a good idea because of how I left. But I really trusted that Tim was a man of his word. He was determined to turn the franchise around. He knew business and he knew quality. I attribute all the recent success with TFC, the Raptors, and the Maple Leafs to Tim. He helped lay the foundation for the teams to get to a point where they're in contention. TFC and the Raptors wouldn't be champions if Tim hadn't steered the car down that path at the start. What he brought to the city and the organization — the success and rewarding the passionate fans — can't be overlooked.

The only things that were the same when I went back to TFC were the crest on the shirt and the fans in the stands. It wasn't the same organization that traded me away; they were different from top to bottom. It was like moving back into your old house after somebody else fully renovated it. All the little things mattered, and all the big things were done big. Everything was elevated. From the cars they used for pick-ups, to the meals served in the canteen at the training ground, to the schedule the grounds crew operated on to take care of the grass. It took a visionary like Tim to say, "Soccer is only getting bigger, so let's get ahead of the curve now and jump on it. Let's start it, and let everyone try to keep up with us."

Signing an English star like Jermain Defoe and one of the highest profile American players in Michael Bradley from A.S. Roma, one of the biggest clubs in Europe, was a huge move for a club that had been seen as a laughing stock by a lot of people. Being reintroduced to my hometown alongside those two was a real "wow" moment. Tim told me his vision, and he actually made it happen. I got to the mic and said I was coming home to deal with some "unfinished business."

I wanted to repair the damage that was done.

I wanted to win an MLS Cup in my city. A second chance in Toronto was a gift. If my career was close to the end, it only made sense that it would end in Toronto.

The 2014 season didn't play out the way I had hoped or the way anyone thought it would. Defoe struggled to adjust to the league. Ryan Nelsen wasn't the best guy to manage players. He went from playing in the Premier League to managing in a totally different country. He was learning on the job how to connect with players in that manager-player way. Nelsen was fired in August, and TFC missed the playoffs for the eighth year in a row. That really hurt me.

I wanted so badly to give my hometown fans at least a taste of the playoffs. I wish I could have scored in front of them again. At least, I got to play in front of them and got to hear them sing my song again. Although the season wasn't filled with the success the club had hoped for, it was a bloody big deal for me. I will be forever grateful for the chance Toronto FC gave me to come back with a clean slate. I just wish I could've written more on it.

I didn't think it was worth gambling on my body anymore. My love for the game had definitely changed, just as the game itself had. When I said I was ready to retire, Brandy didn't want me to quit. She felt like she had one more big move in her. She wanted me to run my body into the ground and fully retire on my own terms. Because she had sacrificed everything and decided to have this big family, she didn't want me to leave the game with any regrets.

"If you hang 'em up, I don't want to hear in three weeks or three months that you got more unfinished business," she said.

It meant a lot to me to retire in Toronto. Captaining my hometown club is one of the greatest highlights of my life. I'll never forget the feeling of putting that armband on for the first time and stepping onto the field with thirty thousand fans singing my name. It was an honour to represent my city and my country.

Every now and then something happens that brings back all those feelings, usually when I least expect it. Witnessing a championship in

2017 brought me tears of joy. When Michael Bradley re-signed with TFC at the end of the 2019 season, his words struck a chord. He said, "I feel so attached to the city of Toronto, the club, the team. What we have in Toronto doesn't exist everywhere. Playing here, winning here, it means more. It's pretty simple. The highs are higher and the lows are lower. But when you spill your heart and your soul into something every single day, the emotion of that, that part is so special. For me, my family, what the club, the city means to us — in the end, this was the only place I wanted to be. When you look at Toronto and you look at Canada, the diversity, the tolerance, how progressive the city and the country are . . . we're proud to live here and we're proud to call this city home."

My love of the game started in Toronto. I am so blessed to have played professionally in my hometown. While it was really special to me to close the book on my career at home too, it was harder than I thought it would be. I went through a series of emotions on the day of my retirement press conference. I didn't want a flashy suit this time. I didn't want a big room filled with reporters who didn't know me or didn't care about soccer. I just wanted to get up there and put a bow on things for my family, my community, and everyone who helped me along the way.

My son Tinashe was three years old at the time. He didn't really know what was going on, but he knew that daddy wasn't quite himself that day. So he made sure to brighten things up for me and the press conference room. He joined me in front of the mic and took over the show. He was grabbing my ears and making faces at the journalists. He hijacked the mic a few times just to yell into it. It made the moment seem less serious, yet more important for me. I had a growing family at home, and now I would get to spend much more time with all of them. My wife and I had a good laugh the next day, watching the highlights of the press conference and reading all the journalists compare Tinashe to Stephen Curry's daughter Riley. She may have been the first one to get the attention at her dad's press conference, but T had the better hair.

CHAPTER 14

KEEP ON MOVING

French footballer Eric Cantona retired at the age of 30. He said in a newspaper interview, "I was young [enough] to return to play and I didn't want to. To avoid that temptation, I didn't watch football for years. It's like a drug and a dealer: if your dealer's next to you, it's harder. Sport is a drug. Your body misses the adrenaline. Physiologically it's difficult to stop, then it becomes psychologically very difficult." He was absolutely right.

It never ends the way you want it to end. Sure, maybe you can name a couple of guys who it worked out for, like Carles Puyol, Ray Bourque, Peyton Manning. They walked away on top, finished as winners. But the list of greats who didn't get to leave on the terms they wanted is endless. I can't imagine the sleepless nights Zinedine Zidane must have had after losing the World Cup Final to Italy in 2006. One of the greatest players to ever kick a soccer ball, a European champion, a World Cup winner, who came out of international retirement at age 35 and carried his country to the final, in what he always said would be his last game ever. And all the world remembers is the head butt . . .

It never ends precisely the way you want it to end.

As an athlete, it's unavoidable, but at some point you have to confront it. Even if you really do want it to go on forever: the lifestyle, the money, the top level you get addicted to performing at. It must end. For some guys it's instant; for others it's a slow burn. I consider myself blessed that my career didn't end that awful night in Panama. It could've. That night, crying in my hotel, alone, I definitely thought it had. But it didn't. I got to play in front of my home fans again. I got to mend and restart my relationship with a great organization, Toronto FC. And I'm home in Canada, working with youth from communities like mine, while my own kids grow up and chase their own dreams. I'm blessed. But the years since I retired have been harder than I ever could've imagined.

My entire career, I always wanted more. I wish I had the mentality to enjoy my success in the moment and be happy. I never really enjoyed it fully when I was playing because I was so committed to the next game, to accomplishing the next goal.

In order for me to be a successful player, it took a tremendous amount of dedication and sacrifice throughout the entire year, not just nine months of the season. I wouldn't rest. In my mind I had to be ready for the next season to start tomorrow. It was an unhealthy obsession; I didn't know how to relax. And it got worse as I got older because I always knew there was some young kid working his ass off to take my spot.

Pro athletes make a living off playing a game. You may think, that's a way to prolong your childhood. I didn't have the average Canadian childhood. I didn't have the average childhood for kids who grew up in my community or others like it, either. Once I committed my life to sports, that was all I knew. Eventually the rewards come and you build a lifestyle that improves as the money grows. It afforded me a lot of opportunities to provide for my family.

The life of a pro athlete is great, but it's also really difficult. There's a lot of temptation. You're surrounded by greedy people. You have to learn how to manage and deal with egos. The game, just like the money, is one element. There are outside forces that can be difficult to manage. It's one thing when they're strangers or what I like to call "opportunity capitalists." But it's another thing when it's family members and friends. You create a comfort zone of "wanters."

When you're playing and the money is there and everything is good, these people want to be around you. When that goes away and you have less to provide, they go away. When you step out of that environment and can't continue with that comfort, it's lonely. What do you do now? You start to analyze who's who. People don't call, people don't come around, people don't care. As much as it's a blessing to remove those people from your life, it's what you've known for years. It's hard enough to maneuver and reinvent yourself professionally, but when you don't know what to do with yourself and you realize that many people who were in your life don't really care about you, it's overwhelming.

I have to admit, when I was a younger player, I didn't have much sympathy or empathy for the guys who spiralled after their career ended. When you're in it, playing the game, living your best life, enjoying success on the field, making money, it's hard to understand how everything can fall apart so soon for a guy. How does someone's 10-year marriage dissolve the year they stop playing? How can you go broke so quickly? I didn't understand how so many guys fell down that road. And then I retired.

One of the things I was looking forward to most was being able to travel with my dad. We always had a close bond. I made sure he never missed a big moment; he was at every All-Star Game and every MLS Cup Final. He was always there and present. When I was playing, we would talk at least every other day. If we went three days without talking, he'd call me to make sure nothing was wrong. Soccer had taken me all over the world, and through coaching youth soccer, we discovered some amazing new places together in retirement.

Dubai is one of the most exotic and unique places in the world. To be in a place so foreign to what we knew and watch him shine in a unique coaching environment was really special. I felt really blessed to be in that space with him, to be able to feed off his soccer knowledge and pick his brain about developing young players.

On that trip, he spent as much time in the bathroom as he did on the pitch. And that just wasn't like my dad. He went to the doctor as soon as we came back, thinking he must have gotten a bladder infection — a common side effect of travelling for a lot of people. The doctor prescribed him some medication and I thought that would be the end of it. A couple of weeks went by and he wasn't improving, so he went back. They shelved that medicine and gave him a new one to try. He finished the bottle and wasn't any better. So he went back to get the next brand of pills. More than two months had passed since our trip. Suspicious that it was something more serious at that point, the doctor ran him through a series of tests.

Stage four prostate cancer.

His world stopped. He could hardly find the words to tell us his diagnosis. I never heard my dad so low in my life. The mental toll it took on him was more aggressive than the actual cancer. I reached out to a contact I knew to get him admitted to Princess Margaret Hospital in Toronto because we knew it was serious. My dad was totally defeated. He never liked needles or doctors or hospitals. Or funerals. This was hell for him.

Since I was retired, I had a bit more free time than my brothers, so I stayed with him at the hospital for the whole week. He couldn't walk, he was so weak. He didn't want to eat the salads and the healthy food I was bringing him. I put my hand on the back of his neck, brought our foreheads together and said, "You know, we're gonna beat this. You've overcome so much in this life. You're gonna beat this too."

I needed him to know that he wasn't alone. Maybe that motivated him because he started to eat better and regain his strength. In a few days, he walked out of the hospital's front doors.

I've always believed that food is medicine, so I made sure my dad had a diet plan and strategies to follow to help him stay out of the hospital. Swapping fried foods and Caribbean treats for salads and smoothies wasn't an easy thing for him. For so many people, food is an addiction. He struggled to stick to the strict diet plan and fell back to his old eating habits. For the longest time, it left him in limbo. The cancer wasn't getting worse, but he wasn't getting better either.

I was religiously driving my dad downtown to the hospital for appointments every two or three days, on top of driving my son Adisa to training at Toronto FC's academy after school five days a week. We lived in King City. My dad was in Markham. I spent more time in the car than most Uber drivers. I didn't have as much time as I needed to invest with my family at home or with my academy and other businesses. I was exhausted. This went on for more than two years before I eventually moved to Markham to be closer to my dad.

I never expected to deal with something like this at this stage of my life. But as they say, "When it rains, it pours." With great joy comes great sorrow. Was the cost of winning all those championships having to endure such suffering later?

Every year has been challenging. I stepped away from something I love, something that had shown me the world, something that had brought me to my wife and countless friendships — so now what? Everything I know is because of soccer.

Every retired athlete gets asked, "What do you miss most?" No matter the sport, the answer is always the same: "the guys" or "the dressing room." That's not a media-trained answer. That's the truth. As an athlete — long before you go pro — you're always part of a team. There's always a *we*, striving to reach a common goal. You go through everything together — on and off the field. When you retire, that's gone. Sure, some guys stay friends for life. Some guys, like me, had big families young, so there's a big "we" waiting at home. But it's not the same. You go from "we" to "me, myself, and I" the second you walk out of that retirement press conference.

At first, when people would ask how I was doing, I had the quick answers everybody wanted to hear: "Yeah, I'm good, things are great. It's different now, but you know everything's great . . . I'm at peace with it."

But really, deep down, the truth was, "Fuck, man, I miss it. And I don't know what to do with myself."

I had a crisis. I had to reestablish who I was. That's a real challenge at 40 years old. At first, I made life fast and chaotic. I grew my foundation and academy and did some positive things, but I wasn't doing everything with purpose. I spread myself thin not because I valued the work I was doing, but because I was just trying to keep myself busy. I would take meetings with anyone just to keep busy — business pitches and non-sense lunches.

I was very disciplined as a player. That's not to say I didn't go out and enjoy myself every now and then. But I never allowed myself to rely on my natural abilities to go wild and enjoy that rookie-type life. I married young and that kept me disciplined off the field. I didn't realize it at the time, but when I retired, I pulled away from my family and sought attention in all the wrong places. I wanted to go out all the time. I didn't get to party as a player — now I didn't have any restrictions. I can't blame the people I was going out with for enabling me, because I made the choice to go out. But I was seeking something that, really, I had at home. I didn't see it because I was blinded by my ego and by this feeling of loneliness. My brother had to tell me to slow down. That was the moment when I started to look at what I was doing to myself and those around me.

Those who have strong family support usually make it out. But those who don't — which is the majority of athletes—struggle. Inner city kids tend to go back to their inner city ways. When you grow up in the hood, you're exposed to too much too soon: poverty, drugs, women. My Aunt Lea mentored me growing up. But I needed her most when I retired. I needed that counselling and guidance that was so valuable when I was young to help me find myself all over again.

My whole life people wanted to be around me. There was always someone looking to catch up or go for a drink. But not as many people pick up the phone to ask, "DeRo, how are you really doing man? How you dealing? How are your relationships?" In that period when your whole world is upside down, you realize who your real friends are. I realized I didn't have as many as I thought.

Very few people knew what I was dealing with, with my father. He was always a very private person, but so well connected. He didn't want people feeling sorry for him, and I didn't want people reaching out with their sadness and fears. Keeping him in a positive frame of mind seemed like one of the few things I could do to help him in his battle. His girlfriend, Rose, played such a big part in helping to care for him and driving him around when my brothers or I couldn't. She had to take a lot of time off work, and she cared for him every night. Bless her heart.

It was exhausting for everyone involved, but nobody more than my dad. He was the one getting poked and prodded, enduring blood transfusions all the time. The chemo treatments took such a toll on him physically and mentally. My dad really loved two things: driving and training the kids. Cancer ridden, he couldn't do that anymore. He was suffering. He would come out every now and then to support, but he wasn't able to coach and really be involved.

Once he got sick, he couldn't look at himself in the mirror. Every time he went to the washroom, he kept his head down, washed his hands, and walked out. He didn't want to see himself like that. He was such a proud man, and not just when it came to his appearance. I knew it pained him to have to ask for help all the time.

I always looked at my dad like this invincible force who could overcome anything and everything. Because that's what he did my whole life. To watch my hero, my backbone, be so vulnerable and get so weak was the hardest part of those three years. It's hard to see someone go through so much pain but still smile and hide their emotions because they don't want the people they love to see their pain. There's a guilt associated with making your loved ones miserable, no matter which side of the coin you're on.

As busy as I was, not having a regular routine left me feeling aimless. Family helped, but for years I had put so much faith in my wife to handle everything with the kids. In retirement, I was there physically and supporting in any way I could when my schedule allowed me to. But that transition to being full-time husband and father was really tough. It was a new dynamic — not just for me, but for everybody. It was beautiful in a sense, especially after spending so much time on the road and missing so much of my children's early years. At the same time, I wasn't prepared for the adjustment. I was doing things I never had time for before. I also had to realize that Brandy needed space too. She was on the grind the whole ride with me. Now I was at home, on her field.

I'd roll out of bed and be mad at the world. Just get up and start a day I wasn't excited for, put on a face around the kids and hope they didn't notice. But they saw it, and though they were too young to be able to explain it, they knew something wasn't right. There was no point even trying to slap on a poor "I'm okay" face with my wife. If I hadn't had the TFC ambassadorship role in retirement to keep me around the club, working on community initiatives and getting me out to games, I don't know how far I might have fallen. I don't even like to think about it, to be honest.

I spent my whole life being led by my dreams. When I retired, I was being pushed by my problems. That's no way to live. Eventually I got to a point where I had to make a decision — just like I did when I chose soccer over the streets. I consciously made the decision to be more positive about my situation. And it's incredible how much easier the days become when you change your attitude. I tell the youth all the time, "*You* are your greatest investment." In retirement, I've constantly had to remind myself of that.

Soccer was always my escape from the things that were really bothering me. It was my stress-reliever growing up. In retirement, I realized that a lot of personal traumas I suffered when I was younger were never resolved. And when I didn't have that outlet — that super distraction — those emotions and feelings were heightened. Sport was the counsellor. How was I supposed to deal now? That's something every individual has to figure out for themselves.

There are so many messages in Bob Marley's music that don't stand out until you really need to hear it. I was running away from my problems my whole life. But you just can't run away from yourself. After a couple of years, I started to see a therapist. I should've gone the day I walked out of that retirement press conference. I knew some guys went to therapy. Some friends suggested I should too, but I didn't listen because I didn't think I would need it. I handled everything else life threw at me, so why wouldn't I be able to handle this on my own? I had that stubborn Caribbean mentality: "Just deal with it."

Some guys told me they went to therapy straight away because they thought they were going crazy. Eventually, I realized that I was low and I needed help. And I'm not ashamed to say that. There was a time when I would've been, because I was in denial. I knew my actions weren't consistent with the life I was trying to live.

Retiring is traumatizing. And there's no correct way to deal with that trauma. It's different for everybody. I kept in touch with a lot of players, and I realized I wasn't alone and that everybody was handling it in their own way. A lot of guys also deal with depression or get sucked into all the vices that tempt professional athletes. Whether it's drugs or women, eating, laziness, sadness, or sorrow — everyone has a story. That's what surprised me when I retired. It's not just a few guys here and there, it's across the board.

Bankruptcy. Divorce. Suicide. The rates for retired athletes are higher than a lot of people realize. Everybody's situation is different, and everyone is affected by different things in their post-playing life. But as soon as I retired, it became a lot easier to see how so many guys before me were plagued by some serious issues. Because I became a statistic too.

After more than 20 years together, Brandy and I separated. Our lives had changed a lot and so had we. Work took her to New York, which allowed our son Osaze to live with her and play at New York City FC's academy. It was a real adjustment for all of us, but one that we were able to make work for the kids.

FIFA is starting to step in and recognize the degree to which players struggle post-retirement. MLS has created an alumni program that will go a long way in helping retired players navigate their lives after their careers. It's so important that these leagues and organizations get involved and show these guys that they still matter. Malcolm X once said, "When 'I' is replaced with 'we,' even illness becomes wellness." Imagine if we taught adults that like we teach our kids about "the golden rule."

In the future, I would like to create an environment where retired athletes can seek counselling from other retired athletes. To have a place where they can be heard and know that they're not alone would break the stigma for a lot of guys. It all starts with you, but it's always bigger than you. When you surround yourself with people who push themselves, it motivates you to be your best. There's another thing — as an athlete you have that extreme drive at every level. And then you retire, and that element that you didn't recognize or really understand in the moment is gone. You need to find something to replace it. For some guys, it's business. For others, it's family. It's possible to fill that void, but you can never replicate what was. That's what makes the transition so difficult at first.

Social media is an outlet that I think has saved a lot of guys because it helps them feel relevant — they post and see others' reactions, and they feel important. But it's still empty, and that's what makes social media a double-edged sword. When you're by yourself at night and your mind starts racing and you realize you're relying on clicks and likes from total strangers to feel valued — that's perhaps the loneliest you can be.

It took me a long time to realize you can't calm the storm. But you can calm yourself. The storm will pass. You will fall many times on your journey, and you will feel defeated. But it's your destiny.

When Eric Cantona described sport as an addictive drug, the reporter asked him if there was another drug. He answered, "Yes, having another passion."

———

In 2012, my dad, my brother Mark, and I launched the DeRo United Futbol Academy in Toronto. We built a great team of coaches who worked with kids of all ages. I'm so proud of what we've been able to do and the talent that has come through our program. Several of our DUFA players have been signed by Toronto FC's Academy, including four in 2019. I can't imagine how proud I will be when I make the drive to BMO Field to watch one of my academy kids play for TFC.

My program is not about developing world-class soccer players. It's about developing better people. Teaching kids how to navigate their way through life as well as they can run through defenders on the field is my goal. Sport science has never been better than it is today, but that only benefits one area of the game. Soccer is only one element in these kids' lives, so establishing strong mental ideals is just as important. There's a lot for kids to be afraid of. It's intimidating to play with other competitive kids. It's scary to push yourself to your limit. It's difficult to find out what those limits are. That is a constant lifelong process.

The earlier we learn that fear kills more dreams than failure ever will, the stronger we can be. Failure really is a mindset. We either win, or we learn. That's a lot harder to understand as an adult, and some people never do understand it. In teaching kids, I find myself going back to something Michael Jordan said a long time ago, "If you're trying to achieve, there will be roadblocks. I've had them; everybody has had them. But obstacles don't have to stop you. If you run into a wall, don't turn around and give up. Figure out how to climb it, go through it, or work around it." I've had to remind myself of that a lot these last few years.

Throughout our lives, it's crucial to set goals and then rise above them. Let your passion, effort, commitment, and willpower be your driving force. That's the only way to get through the obstacles in your way. I tell the kids all the time, zero in on what matters most to you and attack it like a hungry lion.

I want to be at the forefront of soccer's growth in Canada. I want to help bridge the gap with inner city communities and provide more fields, more accessibility, and more resources that can be sustained for years to come.

A winning Canadian national team starts at the grass roots level. "Not keeping score" is a method many organizations use across the country. Some think it's progressive for the young kids because they're not obsessed with the result, so they can just focus on the process. I think that's non-sense. There is a place for that — in house league. But when kids are developing their skills and love for the game, winning and losing is part of that package. You can't remove that element and get the same result. Life is about winning and losing. You get fired from your job, you've lost something. You get a promotion, something you've been working hard for, you've won something. That's the mentality I saw everywhere in the States. "Everything we do, we do our best. And even if it's not the best, you're going to believe it is because that gets the best out of you."

Competitive sports are about being competitive. We have to educate the coaches. When your team loses, they don't need to be scolded. And just because they won, that doesn't mean that everything is good. In the last 30 years, I've watched the American program evolve and small countries like Belgium and Iceland close the gap, and I've learned that we need to do a better job educating coaches in Canada.

Kids should know what winning feels like. They should know what losing feels like at 9, 10, and 11 years old. It's not all about winning, but taking that competitive edge away from them is not something other countries do. In Europe, when these young kids score, they run to their coach and the whole team celebrates like they just scored a Champions League goal. We don't have that same joy and energy. I tell my academy kids, "You celebrate like you just scored the biggest goal of your life." The game is all about joy and happiness. We try to downplay that as a country, and it's become part of our culture. But really, celebration is great.

My biggest goal is to help take soccer to the next level in Canada. But it's as if there's a parasite eating away at this sport, and that's why it hasn't grown to the level it should have by now. It's so divided and segregated at all levels. The old are still in charge and make all the decisions. The game needs to be re-marketed in this country. I know the same can be said about sports in general in Canada, but it's time we elevate ourselves and expect and embrace success. Highlight greatness. Highlight our champions. We're the only country that looks to the States for role models and leaders, but we have them in our own backyard. Ben Johnson did it, so I believed I could do it too. He showed me as a first generation Caribbean Canadian that I could be great. That was the first time a Canadian showed me greatness.

Ben Johnson had all of Canada and the whole world silent for 9.8 seconds. Regardless of what happened after, he sparked something in me and other Canadians who hadn't felt or seen anything like that before. I look up to Canadians I can relate to. Terry Fox, what he did on one leg, was my Rocky Balboa story. Those are the guys who showed me "anything is possible" if you just work at it.

Watching my own kids grow up has me thinking about the future. When FIFA awarded Canada the right to host the World Cup with the United States and Mexico in 2026, I was emotional on so many levels.

I've been an advocate for the sport for so long, and I got to witness that history-defining moment as an official ambassador. The night before the official vote, I was a bit of a mess. I had my doubts because from what I had heard, the North American bid was one that FIFA just couldn't refuse. That shouldn't have made me nervous, but it did. Maybe I was afraid I was too close to the forest to see the trees. In the end, it was the right choice.

I'm the product of Toronto government housing. My kids will never know what that life is like. Their kids should never live that experience either. But so many kids do. Far more children do than you might realize. And that's the problem with the system. Those that are in it are often forgotten. Soccer was so transformative for me as a child, and that's why I am so passionate about ensuring that as many kids as possible have the same opportunities, and even better, than I did.

———

When I was playing, I was encouraged to make a plan for my future. Former Kansas City Wizard and Chicago Fire midfielder Diego Gutiérrez really helped me out along the way. He planted the seed and got me to think about what I would do when I couldn't play any longer. Diego introduced me to Nothing But Nets, a global grassroots campaign that raises awareness, funds, and voices to fight malaria.

We went to Mali with our wives in 2007 to hand out bed nets as part of a United Nations health initiative. It was one of the biggest initiatives in Africa's history at the time, focused on AIDS, deworming, female circumcision, and vitamin E deficiency. I went to New York as a spokesperson for Nothing But Nets and spoke at the United Nations. Secretary of State Condoleezza Rice was in the room when I arrived. We spoke briefly about the project and she had some words of encouragement. To stand in front of all those international delegates was nerve-racking. This wasn't like speaking to the media after a game or being interviewed on TV. I was responsible for convincing some of the most powerful people in the world to help impoverished children who were dying on the poorest continent on the planet. I felt a massive responsibility representing that cause.

I really took to the project because of the devastation malaria causes — killing a child between the ages of one and six every 30 seconds. *Because of a mosquito bite.* When Diego told me that, I said, "What do I need to do?" That shocking number seemed impossible to me. Having kids, I'm sensitive to those things. I've always been very committed to helping youth, so when I heard mosquitos were taking lives and limiting countries' abilities to grow and change for the better, how can you not help?

Seeing the hardships and struggles during my trip to Mali really compelled me to help poor kids in my community and give them a chance at a better life. My brother Mark and I established the DeRo Foundation. At first we started with a North American and Caribbean tour in 2008, "DeRo Football — for fun, for health, for life." We held mini camps in Toronto, Houston, Montreal, New York, New Jersey, Tobago, Jamaica, and Barbados. It's grown over the years and now we work with local community organizations year-round to create programs that teach youth the importance of leadership, teamwork, education, health, and nutrition. We offer after-school programs and training clinics that help kids reach their full potential. Keeping the environment fun and friendly, so the kids are comfortable to be creative and try new things is very important to me.

Just before the COVID-19 pandemic, we hosted the first annual DeRo Foundation Gala dinner in Scarborough. There are so many great people from my community who have done great work and continue to have an impact on the community. I wanted to honour and recognize a few champions who inspired me from afar.

Jamaal Magloire came from a similar background and upbringing as me, and he made something big of himself in the NBA. First as a player, when he was the first Canadian to play for the Toronto Raptors, and more recently as their NBA champion assistant coach. He's always been a pillar in the Caribbean community, supporting the culture with his Toronto Revellers Band. He was given the first Community award. Lennox Lewis reached the top of the boxing world and was one of the biggest athletes on the planet, deserving of the Athlete Excellence award. Michael "Pinball" Clemons achieved so much on the football field as a record-breaking CFL running back and has run through walls for the community since hanging up his helmet. He was voted the Global Excellence Award winner.

I didn't want to limit the honourees to the sports world. Toronto City councillor Michael Thompson always supported everything I was trying to do for the kids and soccer in the community. And he never wanted credit for anything. He just helped because he cares. Michael regularly calls me up to check in and talk. Nobody else of that stature does that, but that's the character he is. Director X travelled the world working with some of the biggest musical artists on the planet, always adding his Toronto flare to his productions. Jully Black is Canada's queen of R&B Soul and a true leader, empowering women with her philanthropic pursuits. And the whole night was hosted by Master T, who did so much for the urban music scene in the 1990s.

But the first person who I wanted to recognize was my Pops. There are so many elders who didn't receive recognition they deserved until after they died. I wanted my dad to stand on the stage with all those accomplished people and know how much his efforts were appreciated and how highly he was regarded. And I wanted to show everyone how much he had done for our community, outside of just soccer. As a big brother on and off the field to so many players, coaches, and people in the Caribbean community, everybody loved Tony D. He was the biggest role model in my life. The Tony D. Community award is the one I will be the proudest to hand out every year.

In an ideal world, I would've wanted him to experience that Gala healthy and strong, instead of suffering in the state he was in. But I was so thankful to recognize the great person my dad was while he was alive. I think that may have been the green light he needed to know that he had done all he needed to do here on earth. Two days after the Gala he went into the hospital, and a week later, on March 11, 2020, he passed away.

That week and a half was all about acceptance for me. He was suffering, and I knew that while death would bring pain for so many of us, it would finally bring him peace. I prayed to God to either take him up to his Kingdom or take away his suffering. It just didn't feel fair to see my father go through so much pain.

Our last conversation was about acceptance. He was so tired and beaten down. I felt it was just a matter of time before he passed. I told him that he had done everything he could for us and that we all would be okay. I knew it was time for him to go be with his parents and our ancestors, in a better place. And as soon as I said that, he fell asleep. I left to pick up my son Osaze from the airport. Originally, I had planned to take him straight to the hospital to be with his grandfather, but something told me not to. There had been so many visitors earlier that day, I just wanted my dad to get some rest. We'd go see him first thing in the morning. My uncle called me at 2 a.m. He didn't have to say a word; I knew why he was calling.

That morning I received the Order of Ontario, the province's highest honour. It had been in the works for months, and I had accepted that Dad wouldn't be by my side for the ceremony that day. I never could've predicted he would leave this earth on that day. As hard as it was to get dressed up and head down to Queen's Park for the ceremony, I knew my dad was with me in spirit. And I knew how proud he was of me when he passed. That got me through the day.

My dad didn't want a funeral. He always wanted a celebration of life. Because of COVID-19, we couldn't even give him that. My world was turned upside down, and so was everyone else's. It served as a real distraction for the first few weeks, but the grief was heavy on my 42nd birthday, when, for the very first time, my dad wasn't the first one to call me to wish me a happy birthday. That was his move. He was always so proud of that.

An important part of the grieving process is looking towards the future. I can't wait for 2026. It will change Canadian soccer forever. Co-hosting the world's biggest event will finally put our sport in the spotlight. The whole world will be watching Canada. That puts accountability on the CSA and everyone in Canada's soccer industry. If we want the sport to continue to grow, if we want to hold our own on the field, we have to step up.

Just look at what the 1994 World Cup did for American soccer. Sure, the TV ratings for MLS and non–World Cup games may fall behind the other team sports right now, but look at how much the U.S. program has improved in 25 years. The world expects the United States to reach the knockout phase at every World Cup. Not qualifying for Russia was a worldwide shock. It jolted the U.S. program to reinvent itself, and preparing to co-host 2026 has already done the same for the Canadian program.

It will be surreal to hear "O Canada" sung at BMO Field or BC Place and watch our Canadian boys go out there and play in a real World Cup match. It will be such a proud moment for me. I also fear it will be hard for me to watch, knowing how bad I wanted to be one of the boys on the pitch while I had my chance. I will be 48 years old when the 2026 World Cup kicks off. Not an old man, but one who still wishes he could be out there. That feeling likely won't ever go away.

My hope is that kids will read this book and think, "I can be like him. I can be great. I can make something of myself and get out of this bad situation." That's why I created the DeRo Foundation. I don't want to create the next DeRo; I want to create a player and person who is even better. I want to promote these guys and celebrate their Canadian-ness. I want them to be proud of the country they call home.

Being a father, husband, and professional athlete was not an easy road. Being pulled from all directions and trying to maintain everything was very difficult. Still, the best decision I made was to start a family when I was a young man. It kept me focused and motivated to continue to train hard for my family. But this decision isn't for everyone. And the demands on your time and your energy are extreme.

As I reflect on my choice to be a young husband and a young father, my message to everyone is: appreciate your family *and* all the obstacles that come your way. The ups and downs really are just temporary. All of it will make you a better, stronger, and more understanding person. A truly rich man is one whose children run into his arms, even when his hands are empty. My children are my greatest blessing in life, and they have saved me.

ACKNOWLEDGEMENTS

DWAYNE DE ROSARIO

Thank you to my greatest inspiration: my father, coach, mentor, Pops, aka Coach Tony D — John Anthony De Rosario. Thank you, Aunt Lea, for instilling a good foundation in me as a child. May you both forever rest in peace. Thank you to the queens in my life: my mother, Carol Ann, for making the sacrifices to uphold the family and for being such a strong, caring mother for her three sons; Rose Cuoppolo, who took me in like her own; my wife, Brandy Oya Bunmi Clark De Rosario, for bringing four beautiful blessings into our world and for holding our family together during my career, with all the travels and hardships that came with it. Thank you to my kids: Asha, Osaze, Adisa, and Tinashe, for giving me more to live for and strive for every day. To my brothers, Mark and Paul, thank you for staying on top of me and keeping my feet on the ground. And thank you to our grandparents, the De Rosarios and the Da Silvas, for playing important roles in our lives. Thank you to Dave Sidhu, Bruce Twamley, Frank Yallop, Dominic Kinnear, and all the coaches I had the pleasure of working with. Thanks for believing in me.

To all my teammates throughout my career, to the "man dem," you know who you are. I give thanks! And thank you to all the amazing fans that supported me, and even all the haters that kept me motivated.

BRENDAN DUNLOP

Thank you, Dwayne, for the privilege of helping you tell your incredible story. Thank you to my brother Sean for being the ideal late-night FaceTime thesaurus, and to Ken Reid for inspiring me at your first book launch with the words, "Hey, when you write a soccer book about the Bundesliga or whatever, I'll be there too." Thank you, Nicky Bandini, Dan Robson, and Kristian Jack for answering all my annoying writing questions, and to Brian Wood and ECW Press for making this happen. Thank you, Sharman, KJ, and Dobby for helping me turn my passion for soccer into a career. And, finally, thank you to my amazing wife, Elena, for supporting and motivating me throughout this long process. I couldn't have done this without you and Sampson.